BASIC WOODWORKING

BASIC WOODWORKING

Alf Martensson

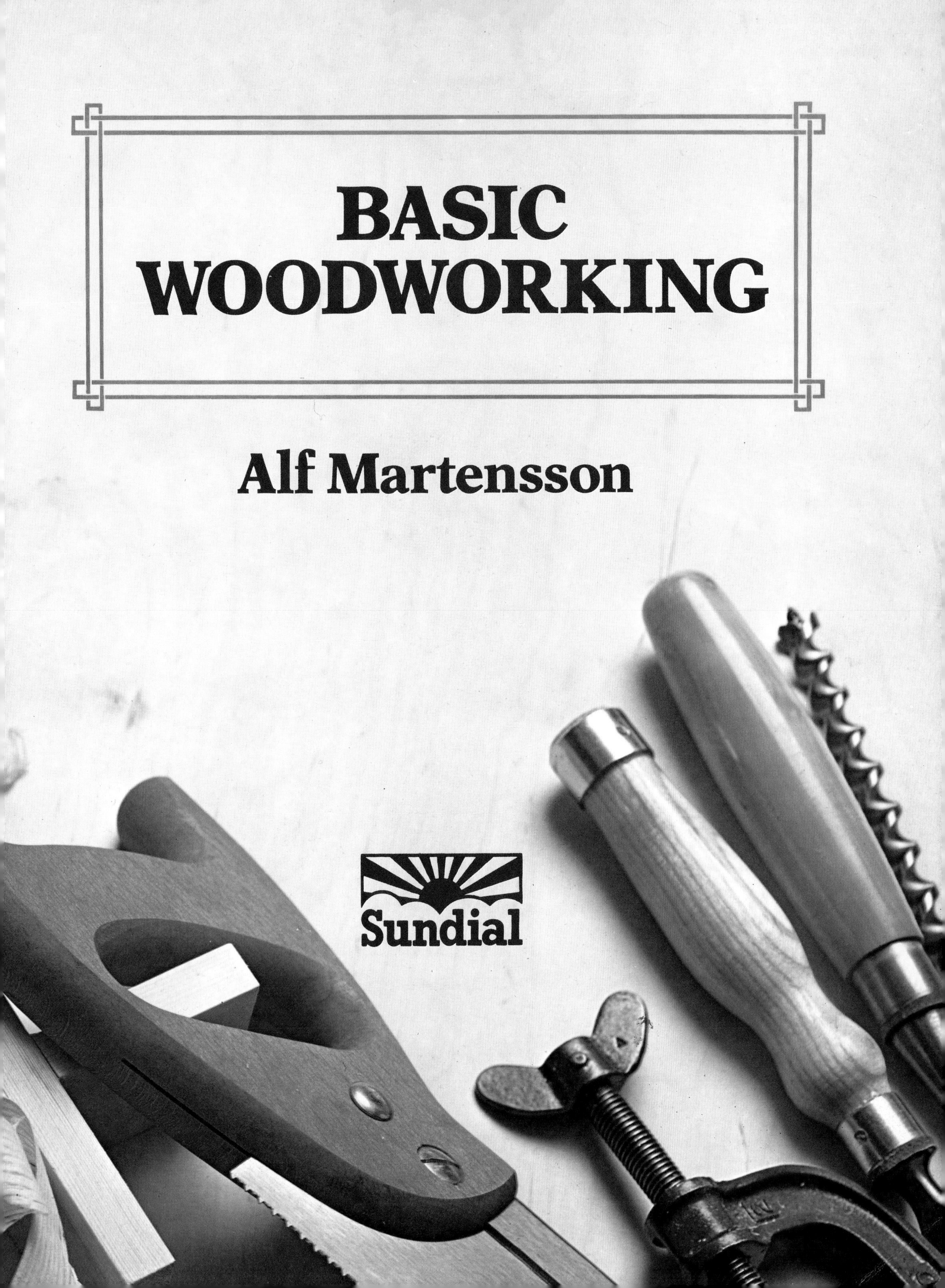

Sundial

Contents

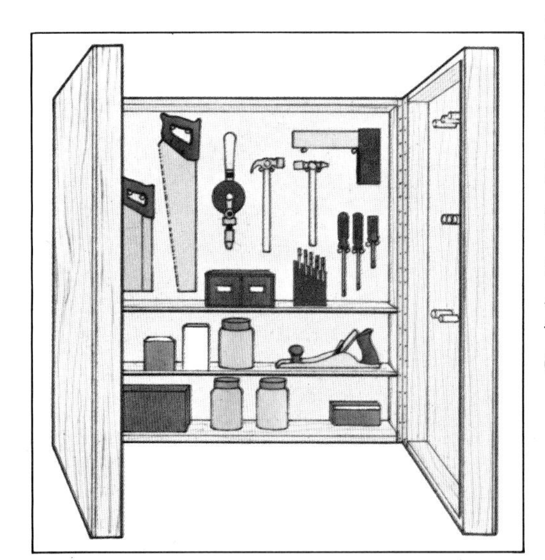

First published in 1978 by
Sundial Books Limited
59 Grosvenor Street, London W1.

Second impression, 1979

ISBN 0 904230 69 4

Printed in England by
Severn Valley Press Limited

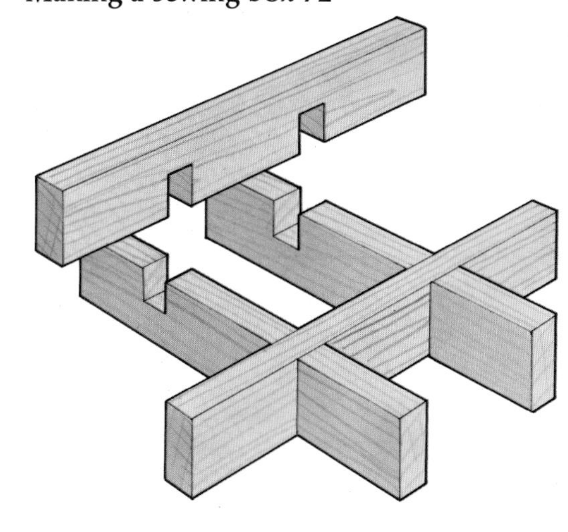

Introduction

Anyone who enjoys making things can learn to work with wood. There is nothing mysterious or especially difficult about woodworking — you don't have to be born into a family of cabinet makers or start learning at an early age to become competent as a woodworker. The most important thing is that you like wood as a material, like the way it looks, feels, smells and finishes and that you want to know more about using it. Understanding the material you are using is an important part of being successful in working with it.

For most of the small projects described in this book, you don't have to worry about expansion and contraction, and many of the other unpredictable qualities of wood. But as you get further involved in making new things and repairing old things you will become totally fascinated with all the various types of wood and their characteristics, history and folklore. You only understand wood by experience, by working with it and feeling how hard it is to cut, how it smells and most of all, how it behaves once the piece of furniture is finished.

A softwood, such as pine for example, which is the least expensive and most easily available timber is very easy to saw, drill and cut with a chisel, because it is so soft. But the fact that it is soft also means that it won't give as smooth or as hard a finish as a hardwood, which is more difficult to work.

Working with wood is an immensely satisfying pastime whether you are making a simple pine spice shelf or fashioning a piece of fine furniture in an exotic hardwood. You will probably get just as much satisfaction when cutting your first halving joint as you will later when doing dovetails.

This book sets out to introduce you to wood and woodworking tools and techniques and to encourage you to learn and practise a variety of woodworking skills by actually making up useful projects such as a shelf unit, sewing box or bench hook.

Most people want to know how to cut a halving joint not for its own sake, but in order to make something which they need. There is just as much emphasis in the book on nails, screws and modern fasteners as on traditional joints to show that woodworking doesn't necessarily have to be complicated and mysterious in order to be enjoyable.

The book sets out to introduce you to wood and woodworking tools and techniques so that when you see something in the shops which you know you can make much better for half the cost you will know exactly what to do. It provides you with the fundamentals that will enable you to get the most out of your tools and to produce good and careful work while enjoying what you are learning.

Becoming a really good woodworker requires time and practice. Good tools are essential — the basic tool kit described on pages 16-17 will help you choose. Learn to handle your tools correctly and safely and discover how to use your hands and the raw materials to best advantage; this can only be learnt by trial and error at your workbench. As always, it is really very simple, once you know how to do it, and you get to know how to do it only with practice.

The simple and attractive projects in this book have been designed to demonstrate some of the joints described, and to give you a chance to make things right away.

Once you have started working with wood, even on this modest scale, each completed project will inspire you to go on to greater accomplishments. So don't be afraid to make mistakes. Your appreciation of woodworking as a hobby will grow in proportion to your effort. The more familiar your tools become, the better the effects you achieve with them will be.

The scope of this book is basic woodworking but the basic techniques, when mastered, will enable you to make almost anything. For instance, a method of using chipboard and metal brackets to make kitchen cabinets is described on page 79; then by using basic dowel joints (page 62), traditional doors can be made for the cabinets. In this way you will be able to use these techniques to plan your own projects.

Basic Woodworking contains the hints, advice and information you need to set you firmly on your way to becoming a capable woodworker: all you need to add is your interest.

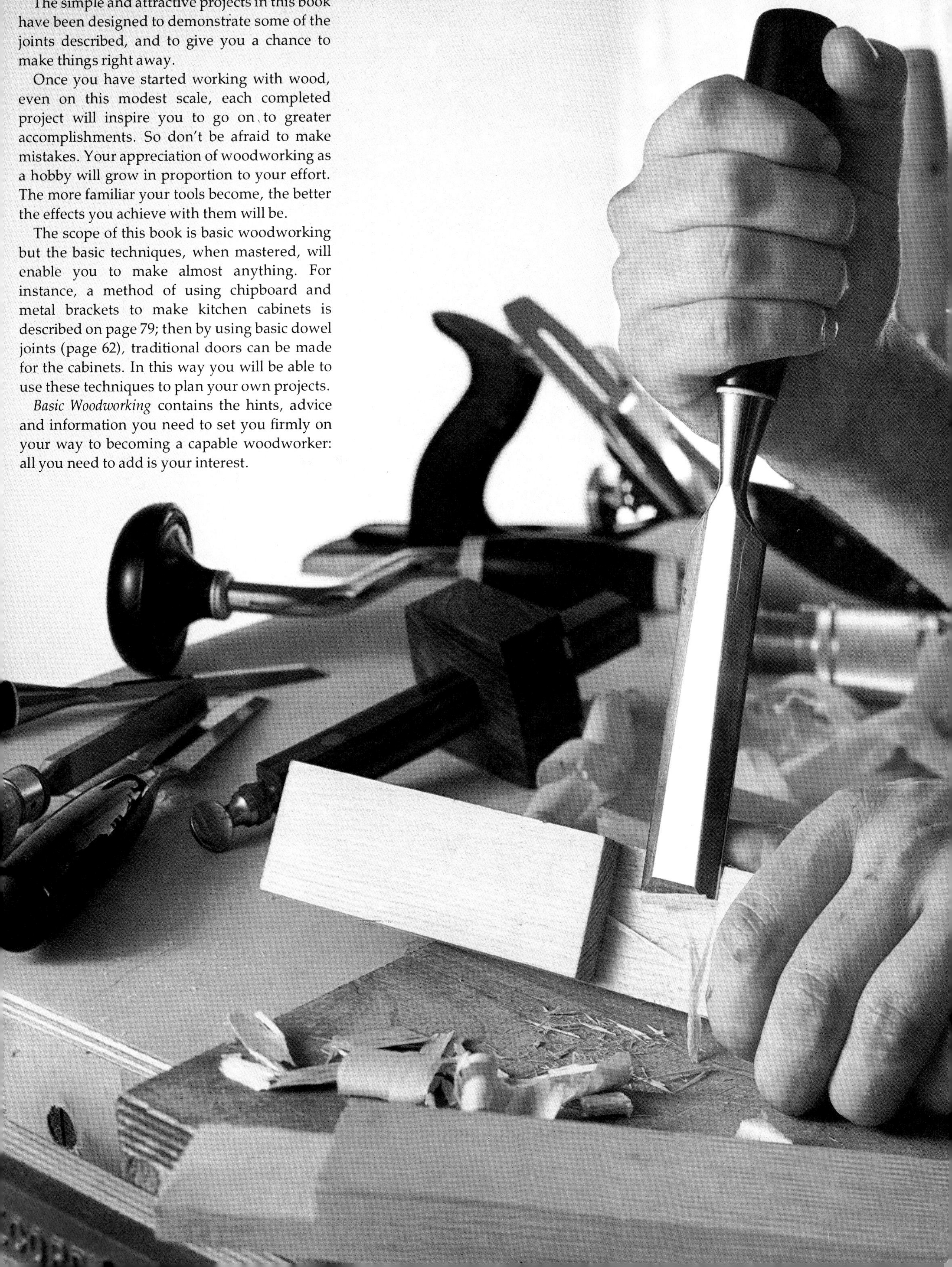

Materials

Tree growth is a very complicated subject but a simplified explanation of the structure of a tree is helpful in understanding what wood grain is, why boards warp, and the difference between softwoods and hardwoods.

Tree growth

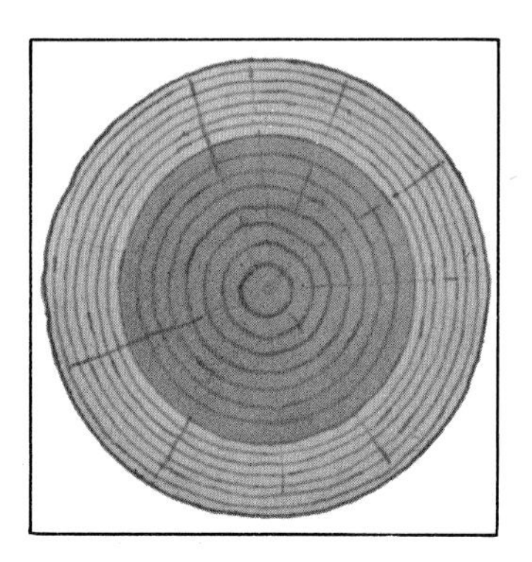

ABOVE: *The annual growth rings in this cross-section of a log indicate the age of a tree. The outer, light rings are the younger sapwood through which the tree gets its nourishment; the darker and more dense heartwood is the older growth of the tree. Just inside the bark is the layer of cells called the cambium.*

OPPOSITE, TOP RIGHT: *Some of the more common faults to look for in timber: warping* **(top)** *which results from uneven drying and which bows the board across the width; knots* **(middle)** *which occur where branches join the main stock of the tree; and splits* **(bottom)**, *called checks or shakes depending on their location, and often caused by uneven seasoning.*

Wood is basically made up of bundles of elongated cells much like drinking straws. It is through these cells that the nutrients from the soil and water travel from the roots of the tree through the trunk to the branches and leaves. The tree trunk consists of the outer bark, a layer of young, lighter coloured wood called sapwood, and the central core of darker and harder wood called heartwood.

Each year during the growing season, the tree adds a new layer of wood just inside the bark. As more sap rises in the spring, the wood produced then has larger, softer cells. This light-coloured wood is called spring wood. The wood which grows during the summer is denser and darker in colour. This difference in colour between spring and summer wood produces the rings to be seen in the cross section of a log, and counting these annual rings reveals the age of the tree.

In general, trees which grow quickly produce wider growth rings and the wood is therefore softer and coarser than that of trees which grow more slowly. Pine, which is a softwood, is inexpensive compared to mahogany, which is a slow-growing hardwood.

Identifying and choosing wood Woods can be identified by their grain pattern, colour and even their smell. Some pines, such as Pitch pine, have a strong resin smell. Cedar has a fresh scent which tends to keep away moths and is therefore ideal for making drawers and chests to store wool clothing.

The hardness and grain pattern is usually an important consideration. Generally, the denser or heavier the wood, the harder and more durable it will be. The grain pattern, however, tends to vary from one piece of wood to the next and should be chosen carefully.

The colour of the wood is also a consideration in deciding which type to use for a particular job. Wood colours vary from the almost pure white of sycamore and holly to the black of ebony, and range from the yellow woods like pine and boxwood, red woods like mahogany and rosewood and the rich browns like walnut and chestnut.

In the end the most important consideration is usually money. Softwoods are fairly inexpensive and widely available in a variety of sizes. Hardwoods like mahogany tend to be much more expensive and are available only at the larger timber merchants.

Cutting up timber When a tree is felled it is usually first sawn into planks so that it can be dried evenly and quickly. There are various methods of cutting up the log to produce the maximum amount of good quality timber. Nowadays, the whole tree is used.

The bark is used for fuel, the sapwood for veneers or for timber, and the heartwood for timber or for chemicals such as turpentine, pitch and tar. Even the chips and sawdust that are produced by cutting up the logs are used to make sheet materials like chipboard and hardboard.

Drying timber There is a considerable amount of moisture in a tree. The weight of the sap can be up to half the weight of the wood. As the wood dries out, it shrinks in width, sometimes up to 10%, and the timber can be ruined by warping and cracks. It is therefore essential that the timber is dried at a uniform rate. To make the timber usable for making furniture or in construction, the moisture content must be reduced to a specified percentage, otherwise the wood will continue to shrink and warp and twist as it dries out. Once the wood is sufficiently dry, it is easier to work and is stable.

The traditional method for drying or seasoning the wood is to cut the log into planks and to stack these with sticks placed between each plank to allow the air to circulate. This method will reduce the moisture content to about 15% which makes the wood suitable for working, but this process can take 2 to 3 years for hardwoods.

Most wood today is dried in temperature-controlled kilns rather like large ovens which quickly reduce the moisture content of the wood to the suitable level. Once the wood is dried it is cut into standard sizes and lengths.

The timber at the local do-it-yourself shop has usually been dried. As long as it is stored in a reasonably dry atmosphere it will remain fairly dry and stable, without warping or cracking. If it is stored in the open, however, it is likely to have picked up considerable moisture and may well warp and twist when brought into a dry room.

Faults and defects As with any growing thing, wood is subject to faults and defects, some of which affect the strength and usefulness of the wood and others which are blemishes affect its appearance only. Sometimes it is these very faults that make the wood more attractive and more valuable: the much prized bird's eye maple with its tiny circular patterns is a defect caused by an insect boring into the wood. Defects are one factor in determining the quality and grade of timber. Wood that is almost free of flaws is sold for cabinet work and wood with knots and imperfections is generally sold for less-finished or construction work.

The most common flaw is a knot, the cross section of a branch exposed in sawing at the point where it starts growing from the trunk. The knot may still be fresh and fit tightly into the surrounding wood. This type of knot is not a problem and can even be an attractive feature of the wood: knotty pine is used as a decorative wall covering. Some old knots, however, tend to shrink and fall out, leaving an unsightly hole in the wood.

Certain imperfections occur after the tree has been felled as a result of uneven or too rapid shrinkage of the wood as it loses moisture. These include cracks along the length of the grain (called checks), splits or separations of fibres along the grain (shakes) and warping and bowing of boards.

Wood has many other faults and it is also attacked by fungi and insects, and these are treated more fully in specialists books, which are usually available at local libraries.

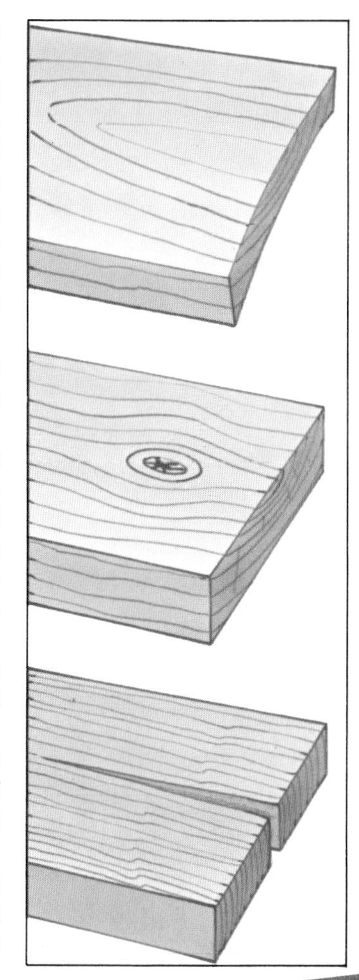

Hardwoods and softwoods

Hardwood and softwood are fairly arbitrary, botanical terms: no real measure of hardness divides the two types of wood and some hardwoods are as soft or even softer than softwoods. Douglas fir is a hard softwood and bass-wood a soft hardwood. Surprisingly, balsa wood, which is the softest known wood, is a hardwood. Generally, hardwoods are more durable and more difficult to cut than softwoods.

Hardwoods are produced by broad-leaved deciduous trees which are slower growing than softwoods, and the wood is usually denser and harder. Hardwoods are more expensive as they take longer to grow, and they are therefore reserved for fine work or are made into veneers. Hardwoods are available in a wide array of colours and markings, from plain solid colours like mahogany to exotically marked woods like zebrawood. Different hardwoods have specific characteristics which suit them for special jobs: ash is flexible and extremely strong and is therefore used for implements which take a lot of wear and shock, such as hammer handles.

Hardwoods which are commonly available through timber merchants include mahogany which is reddish brown and used for fine furniture, beech which is a light wood delicately marked with darker flecks, oak which is light brown and extremely tough, and teak, a warm, dark brown wood which is quite oily and is therefore used for outdoor furniture, draining boards, and for fine furniture. Larger timber yards stock more unusual hardwoods.

Softwoods are produced by trees with needle-point leaves. The most commonly used types are Red Baltic pine, Douglas fir, Parana pine, and spruce.

Softwoods

□ DOUGLAS FIR: reddish brown wood with a pronounced wavy grain pattern. Almost free of knots and easy to work. Used for panelling, construction work, and furniture.

□ HEMLOCK: Pale yellow with a straight grain and moderately fine texture. Used for general-purpose indoor work.

□ RED BALTIC PINE: Light reddish brown wood with even texture and uniform grain. Fairly resinous wood. General carpentry and joinery work.

□ PARANA PINE: Brazilian softwood. Pleasant light to dark brown colour with red streaks. Used for indoor furniture. Easy to work but tends to split when nailed. Virtually knot-free with straight grain. Available in widths up to 300mm.

□ WESTERN RED CEDAR: Light brown wood

These samples of softwoods and hardwoods highlight the differences in grain and texture among the various species. The woods are, **from left to right:** *the softwoods) Parana pine, Western hemlock, Western red cedar, European redwood and (the hardwoods) European beech, European oak, European ash, African walnut, Afrormosia, European elm, Iroko, African mahogany, Burma teak.*

which is resistant to weathering and woodboring insects due to a natural oil in the wood. Will not twist or warp even in heat, but bruises easily.

Hardwoods

□ AFRORMOSIA: Brownish yellow wood used as substitute for teak. Oily and quite difficult to work.

□ ASH: European and North American: Pale yellow wood with fairly straight grain. Tough, and bends without splitting. Used for bentwood furniture, for framing work and for tool handles.

□ BEECH: Fine textured European wood, pink to yellow brown with straight grain. Easy to work and takes nails and tacks easily, so it is used for frames of upholstered furniture and cabinets.

□ ELM: Distinctively grained wood with light brown colour. Strong and durable, but warps.

□ IROKO: West African, similar in appearance to teak. Darkens on exposure to light. Used for joinery work and furniture.

□ MAHOGANY: Reddish wood with attractive grain pattern. A fine cabinet-making wood. African varieties darker and less expensive than those from Central America.

□ MAPLE: Golden coloured North American wood. Nicely patterned, sometimes with bird's eye. Traditionally used for butcher's blocks, as it has no odour.

□ OAK: The two main varieties of oak, European or American, are very strong and dense and rather hard to work. Japanese oak is sometimes offered. It is fine grained, very stable and more expensive than European or American. Oak is used for furniture, window frames, fence posts.

□ RAMIN: Straight-grained timber of uniform light colour used for picture-framing and mouldings.

□ ROSEWOOD: Rich reddish-brown wood with beautiful grain pattern mostly used as a veneer.

□ TEAK: Clear gold to dark brown colour. Hard to work and very oily, so difficult to glue and finish. Weathers to grey colour outdoors if not treated with special oil.

□ UTILE: Similar to mahogany but less expensive. Easy to work and resists decay. Popular hardwood for furniture.

□ WALNUT: Golden dark brown colour with attractive curling pattern, excellent to work and takes good finish.

Veneers

Because hardwoods are so expensive and quite difficult to work, they are often sold as veneers. The wood is shaved into very thin sheets about 1mm thick and then cut into suitably sized pieces or large sheets which are then glued on to less expensive woods or man-made sheet materials. The advantages of veneers in addition to lower cost is that, glued to a stable surface, the veneer will not twist or warp. Many timber yards sell ready-veneered plywood, blockboard and chipboard with matching iron-on edging. The most common veneer faces are oak, teak, and mahogany.

Man-made sheet materials

FAR RIGHT: *Picture frame mouldings, usually milled from an inexpensive hardwood such as Ramin, are available in a wide variety of patterns. They are as marked:* **(a)** *cushion moulding,* **(b)** *spool moulding,* **(c)** *enamelled moulding,* **(d)** *hockey stick moulding (used in the picture frame on page 69),* **(e)** *flat picture frame,* **(f)** *contemporary box moulding.*

There are several types of sheet material manufactured either by gluing layers of veneer together or by bonding wood chips and sawdust into boards. These sheets can be made in large sizes in a variety of useful thicknesses and, if stacked properly, they do not shrink or warp or crack. The common types are plywood, blockboard, chipboard and hardboard.

Plywood

Plywood is an extremely versatile and strong sheet material, used for furniture work as well as for construction. It is made from layers of special veneers which are glued together. Each successive layer is placed at right angles to the one before to avoid any weakness resulting from grain direction. Unlike ordinary timber, plywood is strong in both directions and resists warping or twisting. The layers are glued together in machines under pressure and heat. For exterior plywood a waterproof glue is used. The sheets are then trimmed to standard sizes. The most common sheet size sold is 1220 × 2440mm, but plywood can be bought in smaller quantities by the square metre from local shops. It is available in a variety of thicknesses from 4mm to 25mm. The more plies it has the stronger it is.

The most common types of plywood are birch plywood from Finland, the strongest and most expensive; Gaboon plywood from West Africa, the least expensive; and Douglas Fir from North America, which is medium priced.

Plywood is used to make tables, wall units or cupboards. It can be stained, painted, or varnished to bring out the natural wood grain.

Blockboard

Blockboard is a sheet material with a solid core made of narrow strips, usually softwood, glued together side by side and sandwiched between layers of veneer. The strips run parallel with the long side of the board. It is sold with a variety of hardwood veneer faces such as birch, mahogany, teak and oak.

Chipboard

Chipboard is manufactured from wood particles from both hardwoods and softwoods. Synthetic adhesives are added to the chips which are then heated and pressed into sheets. Chipboard can

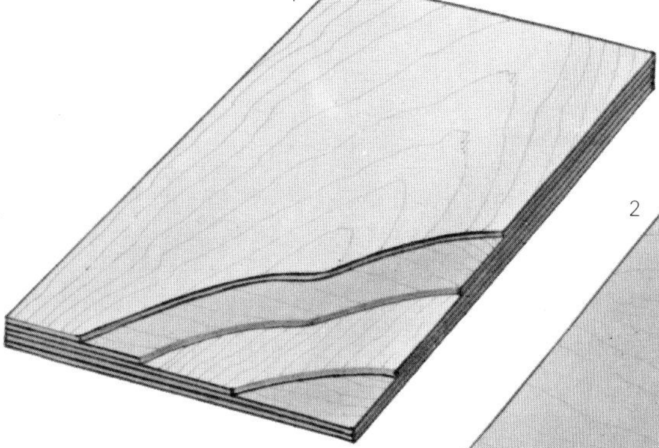

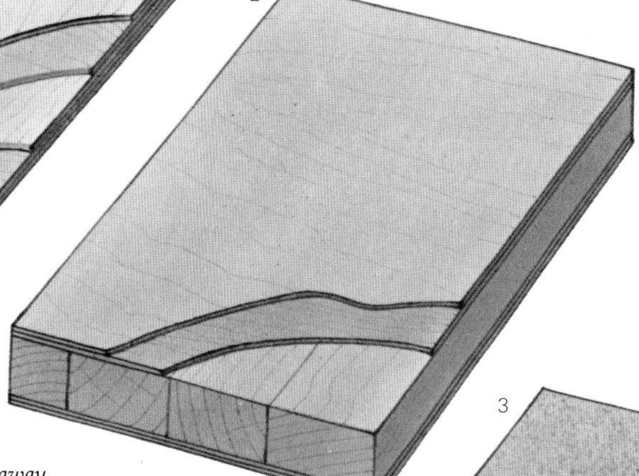

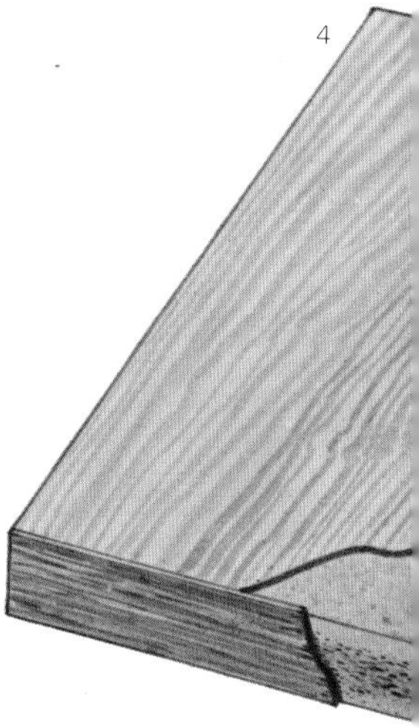

ABOVE, FROM LEFT: **1** *The cutaway section of a plywood sheet shows how successive layers, or plies, are glued at right angles.* **2** *Blockboard is constructed with a solid core of narrow wooden strips sandwiched between layers of veneer.* **3** *Chipboard is made from wood particles and special adhesives pressed together to form sheets.* **4** *Veneered chipboard looks like solid boards of timber and is inexpensive to buy; the sides are covered with a matching iron-on edging.* **5** *Hardboard is available plain, or perforated as shown.* **6, 7** *Tongue-and-groove boards are ready-processed for immediate use.*

be waterproofed with waterproof adhesives, and, as it has no grain, it is a stable sheet, but it is not as strong as plywood or blockboard. Chipboard is available in the standard 1220 × 2440mm sheet size or by the square metre in thicknesses from 9mm to 25mm. It is available in different grades depending on the fineness of the chips used to make it. The smaller the particles the better the grade.

Chipboard is often veneered for use in cabinet work. Most timber merchants sell veneered boards in handy widths with matching edging. Chipboard used without veneer can be sealed with a coat of polyurethane or emulsion paint and then gloss painted, the edges smoothed by rubbing with wood filler or plaster and then sanded down. Chipboard can also be stained with wood tones or with coloured polyurethanes. The stains look very attractive on the flecked pattern of the chipboard.

Hardboard

Hardboard is one of the most useful of the sheet materials for cheap panel work but it is too weak to use on its own. It is a dark brown colour, with one face glass-smooth and the other textured with a criss-cross pattern. Hardboard sheets are manufactured from wood fibres bonded together under pressure and heat without any glue, and is very hard. It is usually available in 1220 × 2440mm sheets in thicknesses of 4 and 6.5mm. It is often used for drawer bottoms, cabinet backs and also nailed to floors as a base for laying tiles and carpets. It is also sold perforated or pierced with uniform decorative patterns for use as a storage pegboard or for wall panelling.

Special sections

Mouldings

Most of the wood you buy will be simple rectangular pieces and sheet material, but specially shaped sections of wood are produced for specific jobs. These sections (mouldings) are used as decorative features for picture frames, skirting boards, cornicework, picture rails, or for a specific function in a piece of furniture such as carrying a sliding door. There is a wide variety of mouldings, ranging from a simple half round to a complex ogee pattern and usually one to suit each job. For further hints on using mouldings on furniture see page 82.

Floorings and claddings

There are two special cross sections for use as floorboards and wall cladding. Floorboards are softwood planks tongued on one edge and grooved on the other which fit together to make the floor stronger and draught-proof. Wall cladding is a finer grade of timber and is also tongued and grooved with the front face planed smooth. This type of cladding is also used for the backs of pieces of furniture such as Welsh dressers. Cladding is usually sold in packages of 20 × 2.4m lengths.

Dowels and rounds

Dowels are round wooden sticks, usually of hardwood, in diameters which range from 5mm to approximately 50mm. They are sold by the metre, usually in lengths up to 2m. Dowels are widely used in furniture, especially chairs, and are particularly easy to attach.

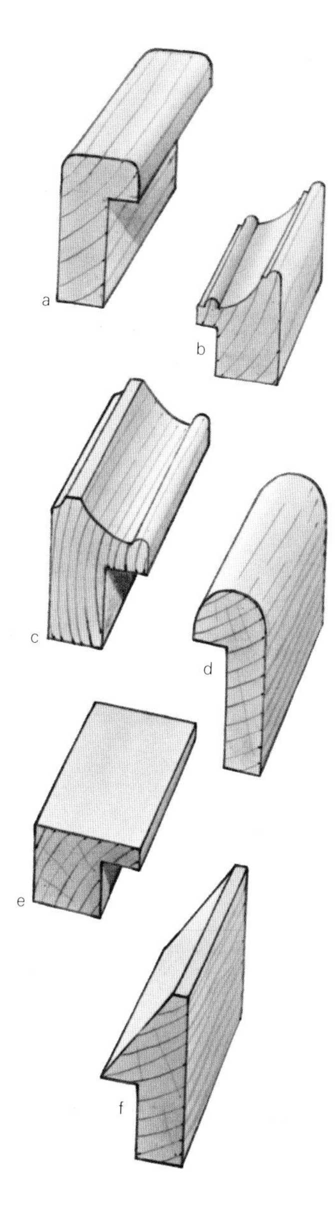

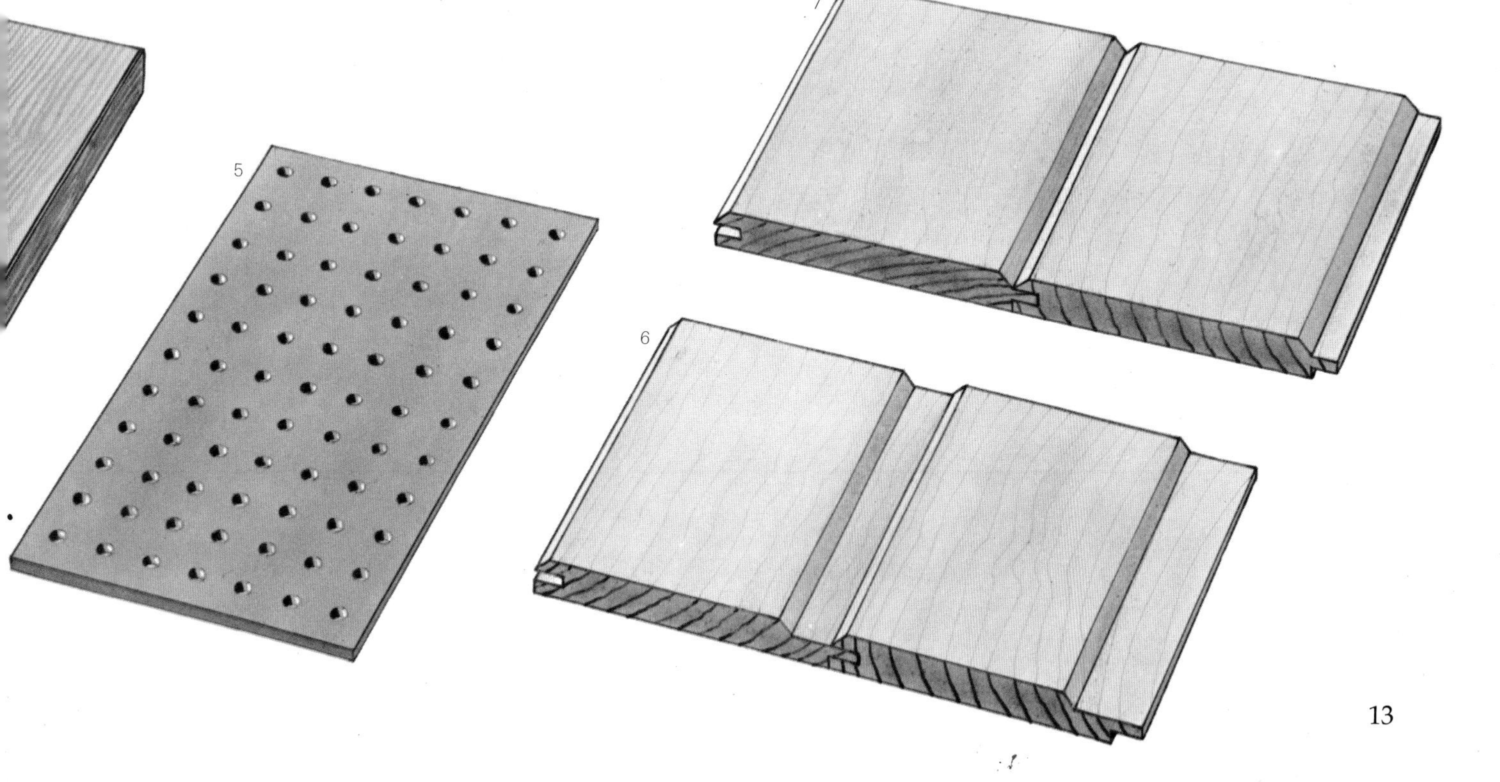

Buying timber

The wood or sheet material selected for a job will greatly affect the amount of work and its final appearance. As the wood is the most expensive item in a project, it is important to choose it carefully and to buy good quality material.

How to choose

First decide on the type of material most suited to the article being made. Fine furniture calls for a hardwood, but a softwood such as pine is excellent for most work. Pine is easier to work as it can be bought already planed, though a few light strokes with a smoothing plane may be needed before finishing. It is much softer than hardwood, and is less expensive. Sheet materials like plywood and chipboard are ideal for making fitted units and work surfaces, where a large and stable surface is essential.

The type of wood will depend on how much money is available; chipboard is less expensive than plywood, and some hardwoods cost considerably less than others. If the wood is to be left natural, your choice will also depend on the colour of wood best suited for the article, and the grain pattern you find most pleasing.

As the wood is expensive, it is important to plan out the job carefully and prepare a drawing or diagram of the finished piece to find out how much material is needed. With hardwoods, as with knitting yarns, the colour of the wood will vary from one tree to another, so it is important to buy all the necessary wood at the same time. Planning the work out will save you the inconvenience of having to buy extra wood or the unnecessary expense of buying too much.

The wood should be well seasoned and dry. Unseasoned wood will warp, shrink, crack and bow and spoil your project. Most smaller timber merchants will allow you to look at each piece before buying it. Inspect each board carefully to ensure that it is straight and true, by sighting along the length. Check for defects and imperfections like cracks, splits and loose knots. Buy wood that is relatively free of knots unless knots are to be used as a decorative feature. It is more difficult to inspect hardwoods, as they are usually sold unplaned and much of the grain cannot be seen on the rough surface of the wood. Never buy wood that has been stored in the open as it is likely to be very wet and will warp. When buying sheet material, check the edges and ends for damage and if they are veneered, check that the veneer is properly stuck down all over the sheet and at the edges, and that the overall pattern of the sheet is pleasing. Boards which have not been stored properly, if warped, should be rejected.

Rough-sawn or planed?

Softwood like pine is sold either rough-sawn or smooth-planed. Buy softwood that is already planed for anything other than construction work; although it costs more, it saves planing time and also enables you to inspect properly the boards.

Timber is sold according to the nominal dimensions. Some wood (about 3mm) is shaved off in the planing process. A 100 × 50mm board, for example, would have an actual size of 97 × 47mm after planing. Planed softwood is referred to as P.A.R., "planed all round". It is important to keep this in mind when planning the dimensions of your project. If you need the timber to be finished to an exact thickness, it may be better to buy the boards in the next thickness and plane them yourself to the desired size.

Cutting to size Timber is sold in standard sections in thicknesses generally from 16mm to 50mm, in widths from 16 to about 300mm, and in lengths to about 6-7m. Shorter lengths are sold by the metre by local timber merchants. Sheet materials are sold in a standard 1220 × 2440mm size or as half or quarter sheets. Some timber merchants are prepared to cut up sheet material for you which makes it easier to transport and eliminates the need for a domestic saw. Bring a detailed cutting list of the pieces you will need with you and a try square to check that the pieces are cut at right angles.

Many timber merchants will deliver a reasonably large order at no extra charge, and some provide regular customers with discounts. Smaller merchants do not usually have facilities for delivery, but they are very helpful in cutting up pieces or in supplying offcuts which are easier to carry home.

Wood is expensive so plan carefully to reduce waste. If you need, say, four 1 metre long pieces, it is better to buy one 4.2m length than two 2.2m lengths. Larger timber merchants will usually not cut off short lengths but their prices are lower than those at most local shops. Find out which lengths are available before assessing the cutting cost.

Softwood is sometimes sold in two grades: joinery and construction. If the wood is not going to show, such as at the back of cupboards, use the cheaper construction grade.

Other sources of timber

Old furniture, such as wardrobes, which can often be bought cheaply at sales, are a useful source of dry, planed hardwoods like oak and mahogany. A heavy coat of varnish may hide some beautiful boards. Remove the varnish by sanding or planing and the wood can be used for other projects. Check carefully that all nails and screws are removed as these can damage your tools such as saws and chisels.

OG ARCHITRAVE
DECORATIVE WALL PANELS
WOODGRAINS – COLOURS
HARDBOAR

Tools and their uses

Woodworking requires a vast array of special tools and devices. The most sensible approach for the beginner is to buy only the tools that are absolutely necessary. One tool can often be substituted for another: a combination square can serve as a marking gauge or even as a depth gauge and it is perfectly all right to use a large nail sharpened to a point instead of a centre punch.

Woodworkers tend to be very fussy and pedantic about tools and techniques, often for a good reason, but it frequently inhibits people who want to make a few things around the house with their limited selection of tools. What is ultimately important is that the finished article is produced with no loss of personal safety.

Always buy the very best tools you can afford; it is false economy to buy a cheap tool, which will neither last long nor do the job well. Most good quality tools last a lifetime if they are properly stored and looked after.

The use and care of tools is covered in the relevant sections of this chapter.

Basic tool kit

1. COMBINATION SQUARE. For use as ordinary try square and also to mark 45° mitres. Can serve as a substitute for a marking gauge and as a depth gauge. The 300mm long steel ruler can be used separately as ruler or short straight edge.
2. TAPE MEASURE. Buy a retractable one with a locking mechanism. 3m length is most versatile.
3. LEVEL. A 600mm long one is adequate for most jobs. For occasional use a less expensive type is adequate. For accurate work a 1.2m metal level is excellent.
4. VICE. If you have an old workbench or plan to make the one shown on page 48, buy a sturdy

6

1

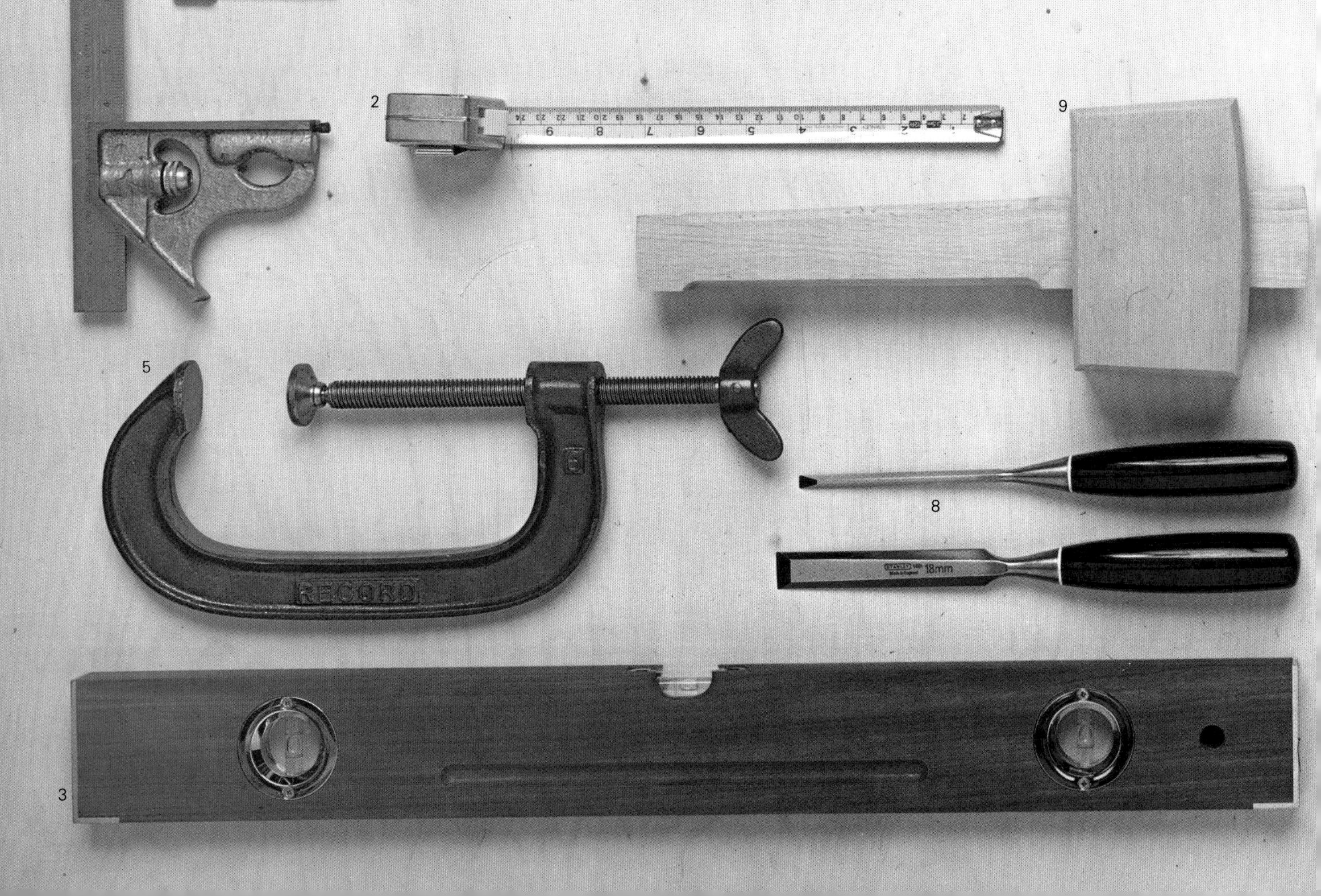

woodworker's vice which bolts permanently to the workbench. Alternatively buy a smaller vice which can be clamped temporarily to the edge of a table or bench. Although it will not hold large pieces of wood, it will suffice for most work.

5. G-CRAMP. Invaluable for clamping glued joints, repairs and holding work to bench. Buy at least one 150mm size.

6. TENON SAW. A 250mm, 14-point saw is useful for all small sawing jobs. For cutting large pieces or plywood, buy a larger panel saw or power circular saw.

7. BENCH HOOK. Indispensable for holding small pieces when sawing. Follow instructions on page 23 for making your own.

8. CHISELS. Start off with two bevel-edge chisels, 6.5m and 19mm sizes. Add 12mm and 25mm later.

9. MALLET. A wooden mallet for use with chisels (in a pinch use a hammer, but only on tough plastic chisel handles). Also for tapping wood joints together.

10. ELECTRIC DRILL. The current low prices for power drills make these a better buy than a hand-drill and a brace. A two-speed hammer action model can be used in masonry and wood.

11. DRILL BITS. One set of carbon steel twist drill bits up to 6.5mm diameter. One countersink bit (high speed type for use in electric drill). Buy larger flat bits or accurate dowel bits as they are needed.

12. BLOCK PLANE. A small plane with a blade set at a low angle for cutting across end grain. Useful for trimming off sawn ends of boards, for bevelling edges and many other small planing jobs. Buy this as a first all-purpose plane and add the smoothing plane later.

13. SMOOTHING PLANE. A 250mm long general purpose plane for straightening board edges and other general work, such as planing off a door or window to fit.

14. SHARPENING STONE. Buy a combination oil stone for sharpening chisels, plane blades, and other cutting tools. See instructions on page 27 for making a box to hold the oil stone. A honing guide is also very useful, though not necessary, to sharpen blades at the correct angle.

15. HAMMER. First buy a general purpose claw hammer for driving and pulling nails and pins. Later add a pin hammer for work with small pins.

16. NAIL-PUNCH. For sinking pin heads below wood surface.

17. SCREWDRIVERS. Start with one small screwdriver for small delicate jobs and a large one for general work. Later buy a useful pump action ratchet screwdriver with interchangeable points.

18. SANDING BLOCK. An inexpensive cork sanding block for use with glasspaper in finishing wood.

19. FILE OR RASP. Not essential, but very useful for rounding and smoothing corners and edges.

20. PLIERS. Again not necessary, but a versatile tool which can be used for many jobs besides woodworking.

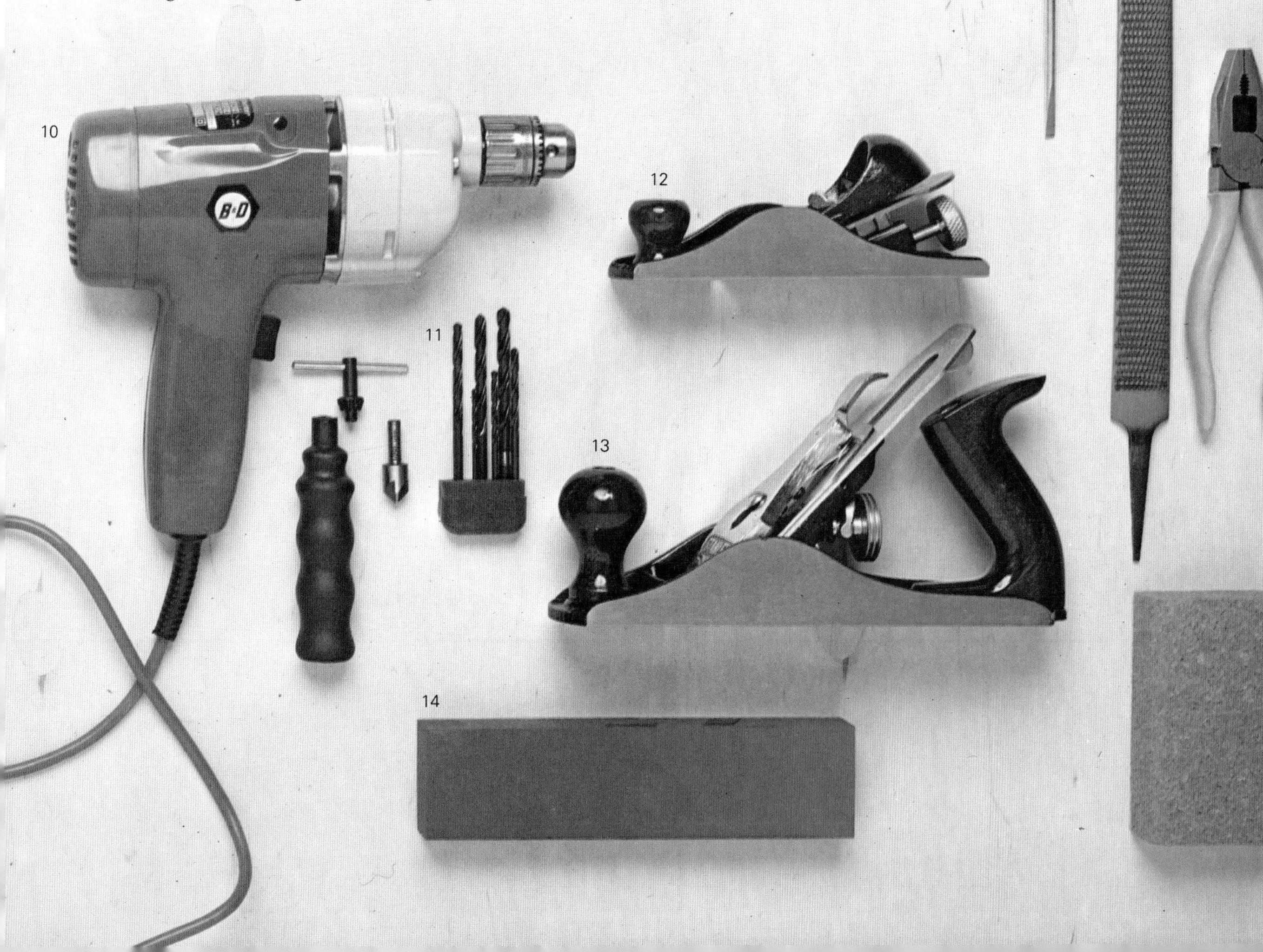

Marking and measuring

A good selection of measuring and marking tools is essential in a workshop. For even the simplest job it is very important that the timber is measured accurately and that the ends are square. You will need a try-square, marking gauge, straight edge, level, steel tape and pencil for most work.

The first step in any project is to check that the pieces are square and straight, then measure and mark them before sawing or planing.

The degree of accuracy required varies with each job. For rough carpentry work the sides do not have to be exactly square and the length can be a few millimetres off. For finer work, measure with a ruler and use a marking or trimming knife rather than a pencil to mark the pieces. The cutting line marked by the knife is thinner and therefore more precise than a pencil line. Use a finer tenon saw to cut the pieces.

Try-square A try-square, available in various sizes up to about 300mm, is used to mark right angles. This is referred to as "squaring-off" for sawing or planing wood. It is also used to check that sections of wood have true 90° angles and square ends. Mark the wood with a sharp pencil or a marking knife, which scores the wood for more accurate sawing.

Combination square The combination square is a useful though less accurate substitute for the try-square. Use it to mark 45° mitres as well as 90° squares. It is also a handy substitute marking gauge, or a depth gauge to measure, for example, the depth of halving joints.

Marking gauge The marking gauge is the traditional tool for marking a line parallel to the edge. Set it to the required width, then run the pin along the surface to score a fine parallel line. The marking gauge is very useful in making wood joints such as halving joints or mortise and tenon joints, because the line scored makes an accurate starting guide for the chisel.

Straight edge It is essential, especially when working with large sheet materials such as plywood, to use an accurate straight edge for marking and checking that pieces are square. Buy a 1m steel ruler or make a straight edge out of, say, a piece of sturdy plywood which you

LEFT: *To ensure that the line you draw will be at right angles to the edge of the board, hold the stock of the try-square firmly against the timber.*

know to be straight. Indicate the straight edge with a mark and hang it within easy reach.

Compass Mark circles with a compass, or for large circles, a piece of string fixed with a pencil to one end. For small diameters, such as those used in rounding corners, use a household tin, plate, jar lid or whatever is handy, as long as it has roughly the correct radius.

Level Check that surfaces are horizontal or vertical with a level. Adjust one end of the surface until the air bubble is centred between the small marks in the level.

Rules and measures Measure lengths with a ruler or a tape measure depending on the job. For short accurate measurements, such as the exact width of a board, it is better to use a steel ruler with fine gradations but in practice, most woodworkers use a tape measure for all measurements. The small hook on the end of the tape may work loose with age, and it is important occasionally to check the accuracy against a steel ruler. Use the steel tape measure for long measurements with one end held by the hook on the edge of the wood. For internal measurements allow an extra 50mm to allow for the width of the steel case.

Hammers and mallets

OPPOSITE: The wooden mallet allows you to control taps as you chisel out a joint such as this mortise and tenon, and it is safe for the wooden handles.

*OPPOSITE BELOW: **1** The claw hammer is used to pull out nails, but always remember to protect your work with a scrap of wood or piece of cardboard. **2** A handy trick for driving in small nails and panel pins is to push the pin through a piece of sturdy cardboard so that you have something to hold on to. **3** A nail punch makes it possible for nails and pins to be set below the surface of the timber; the holes can then be filled and sanded smooth.*

A hammer is a basic part of any tool kit. It is designed for driving in and pulling out nails but in practice it is also used for various jobs, such as tapping on a screwdriver to loosen a hard-to-remove screw.

Claw hammer The general purpose claw hammer, with a steel or wooden handle, is available in various weights and it is important to choose one that is comfortable for you. Use a claw hammer to drive in most large nails. Grip it near the end and start the nail with a few light taps, then progress to harder blows. It takes a little practice to drive nails without bending them.

Keep the face of the hammer bright and clean by rubbing it on fine glasspaper. It is much easier to drive in a nail straight with a clean hammer face.

To pull out nails with a claw hammer put a block of wood under the head to get better leverage and to protect the surface underneath.

Cross-pein or pin hammer Most woodworkers use a cross-pein or a Warrington hammer on smaller nails and especially on panel pins. (See page 52 for descriptions of nails and pins.)

The cross-pein hammer is used with a light touch to prevent the delicate panel pins from bending. To drive in very short, difficult-to-hold pins, start with the finer cross-pein and then finish with a few taps from the face end. Alternatively, use a piece of cardboard to hold very short pins in place for hammering. Push the pin through the cardboard and hold the edge of the cardboard until the pin is well-hammered in before tearing it off.

Nail punch Panel pins can be sunk in wood by driving the small heads below the surface with a nail punch. Nail punches are available in various sizes with points from 1.5 to 4.5mm in diameter to match various sizes of pins. Drive in the pin with a hammer, leaving the head just above the surface of the wood to prevent damaging it with the hammer. Hold the punch firmly on the head of the pin and drive it below the surface with one or two light taps. Fill the small hole with woodfiller coloured to match the wood and sand it smooth.

Wooden mallet The steel head of a hammer could damage or dent chisel handles, particularly wooden ones. A wooden mallet, usually made of beech, is used instead of a hammer. Although the mallet is quite large and robust it can be used to produce very delicate work. It is quite easy to control a chisel for making a cut such as a halving joint by using a few light taps with the mallet. Professional woodworkers also use a soft rubber-faced hammer to tap together wood joints and to adjust glued-up frameworks. The soft face leaves no marks on the wood. For a home-made substitute, tape several layers of cardboard to the face of your mallet. This will soften the blows and allow you to tap home stubborn wood joints without marking the wood and causing unsightly marks.

BELOW, FROM LEFT: The claw hammer is an all-purpose tool for driving and pulling out nails but is too heavy for working with panel pins and lightweight nails. The lighter pin or cross pein hammer is best suited for this work. A wooden mallet is not essential as you can hold a piece of scrap wood between the hammer and the work, but it is useful for chiselling as it does not damage the handles of the chisels.

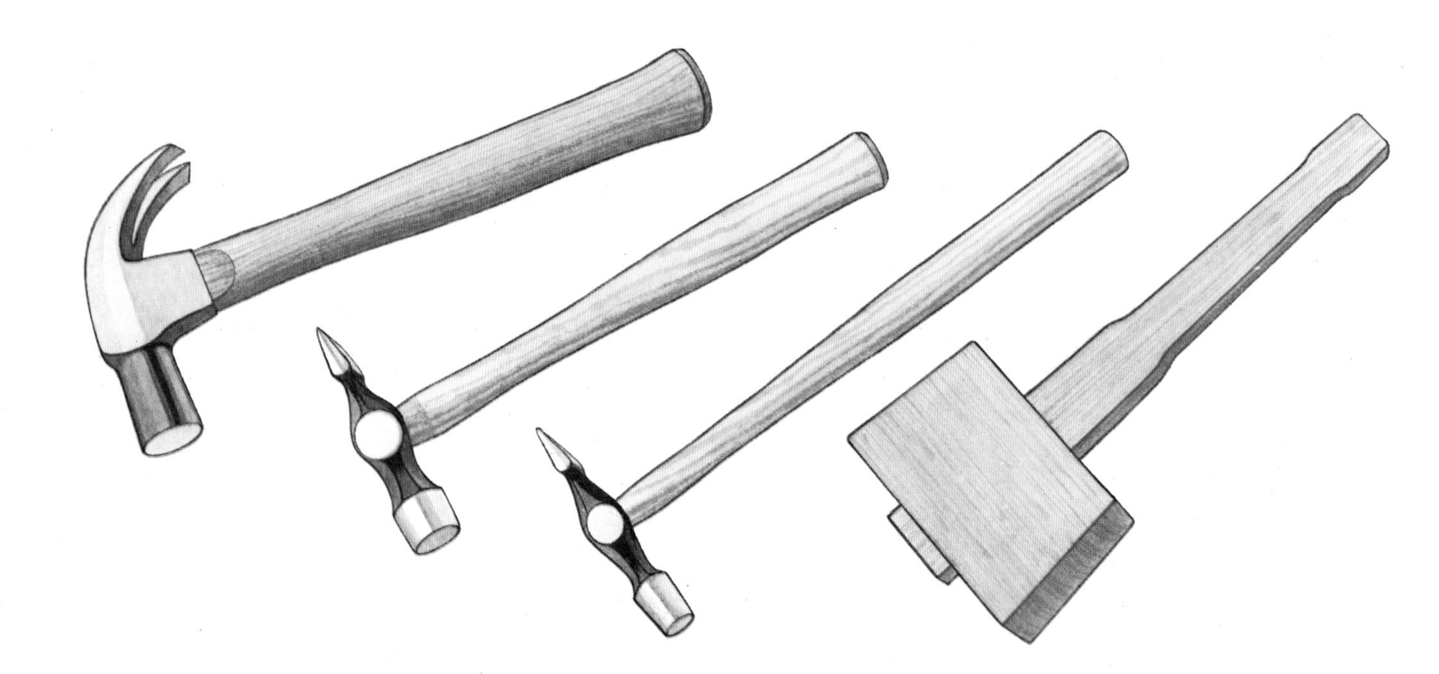

1
2
3

Saws

Saws are used for cutting with the grain (ripping) or cutting across the grain (crosscutting). Think of the grain as bundles of drinking straws; it is easy to see that the action of cutting along the grain is very different from cutting across it. The teeth of the saw do the cutting and basically it is the number of teeth per 25mm that determines the type of cut the saw makes. The more teeth there are, the finer the cut. A rip saw has about 6 teeth per 25mm (referred to as 6 points) whereas an extremely fine dovetail saw may have as many as 32 points per 25mm.

Sawing is quite easy with a little practice. It is most important to use a sharp saw: it is difficult, even for a professional woodworker, to saw straight and cleanly with a dull saw. A dull saw is also dangerous, because you tend to force it and lose control of the tool. If in doubt about a saw's sharpness, send it to a "saw doctor". Large hardware shops usually offer this sharpening service for a reasonable price.

You can manage with one or two saws when you first begin woodworking, but a wider range will make your work easier. The large panel saw **(1)** *serves as an all-purpose tool for both ripping and crosscutting. The smaller tenon or back saw* **(2)** *is reinforced along the back with a steel or brass bar. There is also a special back saw* **(3)** *for cutting dovetails. Coping saws* **(4)** *and fret saws* **(5)** *are used for cutting irregular shapes or for cutting out interior areas of a board.*

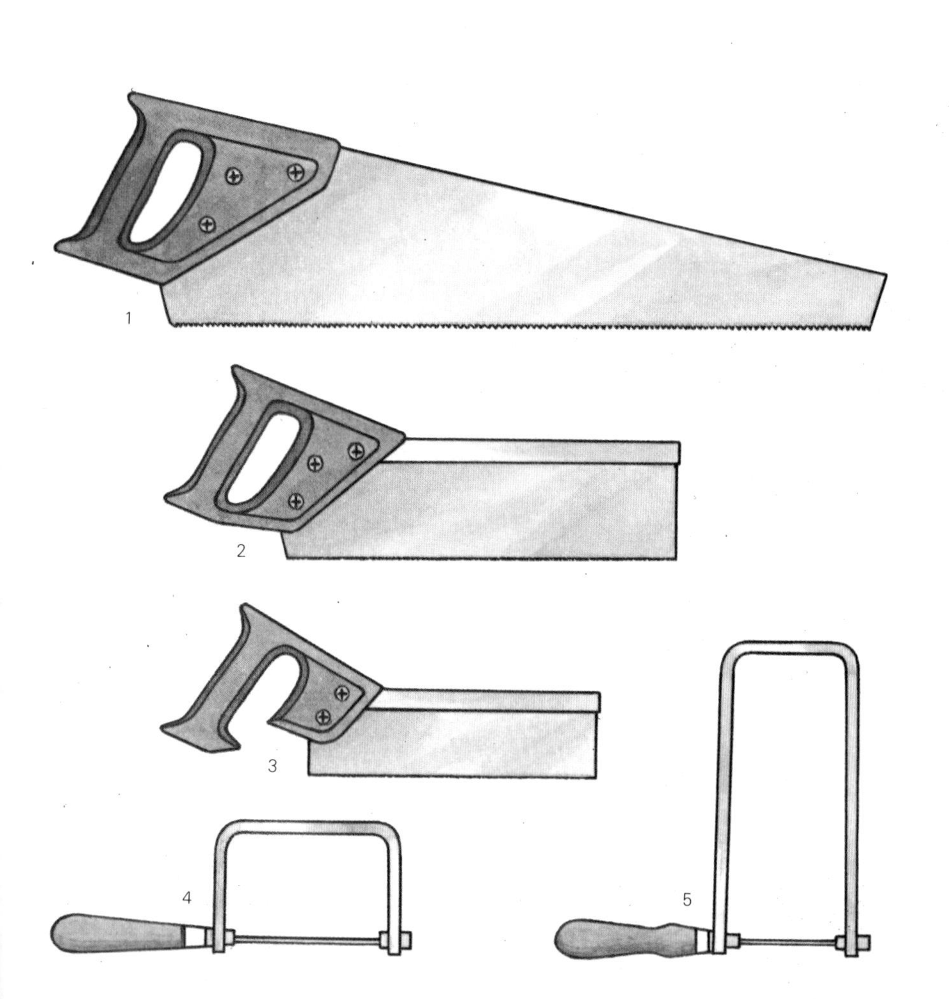

General purpose saws

The larger rip and crosscut saws are about 600mm long and are used for rough cutting of larger pieces of timber. The panel saw is a combination of the two and the best general purpose saw to buy. It is particularly useful for cutting up large panels of plywood, hence its name.

Using a panel saw Hold a panel saw with the index finger pointing along the handle for better control. Start the saw cut with a few light strokes, carefully using the thumb of your free hand as a guide, then use long, firm strokes to saw the wood. Remember that saws cut only on the downward or "away" stroke.

Support the wood while sawing on a couple of trestles, easily made by nailing together offcuts (see page 44 for instructions). Give extra support to large panels of plywood or chipboard by placing two or three boards under the panel on either side of the saw cut. Remember that the saw removes a 2 to 3mm width of wood called the "kerf", so if you saw along the centre of the line you will end up with a smaller piece than you measured for. Instead, always saw on the *waste side* of the marked line so you cut off a piece of the exact dimensions you want. Leave a bit of extra waste if you intend to finish exactly to the marked line by planing off.

Using a rip or crosscut saw The panel saw is designed more for cross-cutting than for ripping. For ripping long and thick boards it may be better to buy a special rip saw, or alternatively to use a portable circular saw.

In ripping, saw along the waste side of the line, supporting the board on two trestles, cramping it down to hold it steady if necessary. To prevent the saw jamming on long cuts, wedge a small piece of wood in the cut as you proceed to separate the pieces and make it easier to saw.

Similarly, in crosscutting support the board on the trestles or on the bench with the part to be sawn off protruding. Saw with long even strokes and remember to hold the off-cut before it falls off, otherwise it may tear the wood as it hangs.

Using a tenon saw The tenon saw is a small crosscut saw with the top of the blade stiffened with a piece of brass or steel to keep it straight. It is the best saw for small, accurate work.

Buy a 14 point, 250mm long tenon saw and use it, with a bench hook, for cutting small pieces and also for cutting wood joints, such as halving or mitre joints. For best results hold the work firmly in the bench hook or cramped to the bench, if necessary, and saw with firm, even strokes using the full length of the blade. With a little practice clean accurate cuts can be made easily with no need to plane off afterwards.

Project: Making a bench hook

Drill two countersunk clearance holes for the screws in each length of 25 × 50mm batten. Locate the first 25 × 50mm along the back edge of the square base, drill the pilot hole in the base, add glue and screw the batten to the base. Turn the base over and repeat for the back edge of the other side.

To use the bench hook, place it with the bottom batten against the edge of the work bench. Hold the piece to be cut firmly against the other batten, then saw, using the edge of the base as a guide.

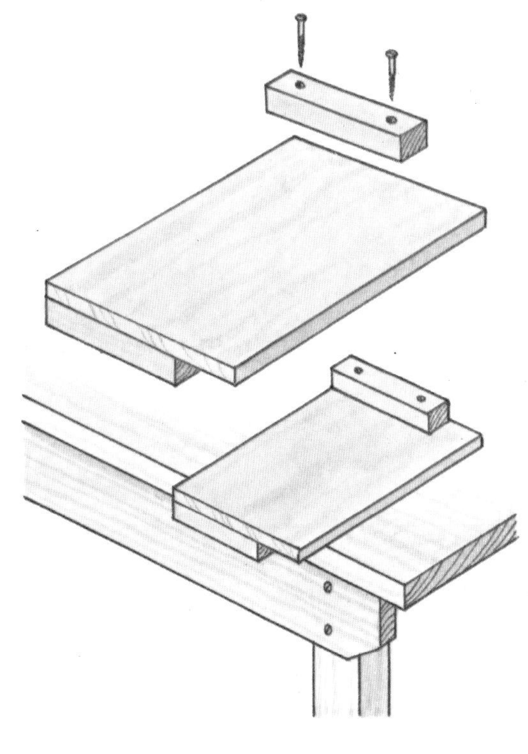

RIGHT AND ABOVE: *A bench hook is used with a small saw, such as the tenon saw, for cutting small pieces of timber accurately. It also provides a stable base for holding the work. This bench hook is made from three pieces of hardwood or plywood which have simply been glued and screwed together. You can countersink the screws and either fill the holes with matching plastic wood or with a wood plug for a more professional finish (see page 85).*

Bench hook

Things to buy

One piece of 20mm thick hardwood or birch plywood, approximately 250 × 250mm
Two pieces of 25 × 50mm hardwood (use softwood as alternative), 200mm long
Four No. 8 countersunk wood screws, 32mm long
Woodworking glue

Tools needed

Drill and drill bit, countersink bit
Screwdriver

Using a coping saw and fret saw Curves are sawn with a coping saw or a fret saw.

The coping saw is the more common of the two. It is used frequently in a workshop for cutting various curves in the wood up to about 25mm thick. To fix the blade, first unscrew the handle a few turns to loosen the tension. Fix the top end of the blade in place, teeth usually pointing towards the top and, holding the saw against the bench with the handle against your body, force the ends of the saw together to fix the blade in place. Finally tighten the handle. The blade of the coping saw can be rotated with the direction of the cut.

To cut a curve, place the wood in a vice or on an easily made holder. Start the cut and stop, if necessary, to change the blade direction as you cut around the curve.

To make an internal cut, first drill a hole within the marked out waste area, then undo the blade and thread it through the hole before doing it up again.

The fret saw has a much larger neck and can therefore cut further in from the edge than the coping saw. It is used for finer, more intricate work such as making models and jig saw puzzles.

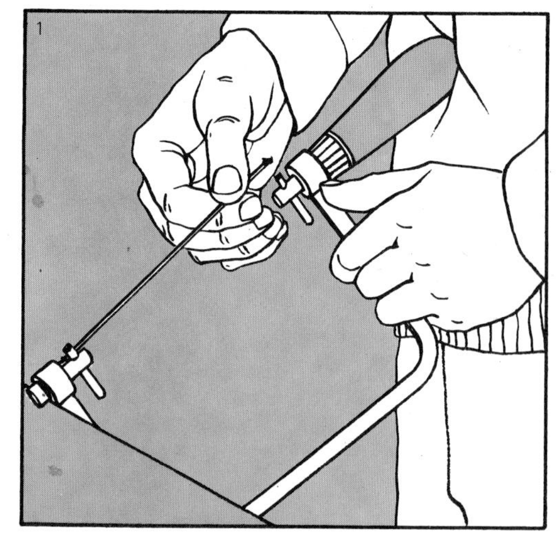

Caring for your saws

Saws must be kept sharp. A blunt saw is difficult to use and can be dangerous, and should be sharpened regularly. If you saw through a nail your saw will undoubtedly need sharpening. This job can be done at home with files to sharpen the teeth and a special "saw set" to set each tooth at the required angle, but it is much easier to send your saws to a "saw doctor" who will do the job expertly. Ask at your local hardware shop. They usually make a small charge for sharpening saws. It is worth doing often, as it is much easier and better to work with a sharp saw.

To store saws, hang them up by their handles in a cabinet or on the wall. Occasionally wipe the blade down with oil to prevent it from rusting, and keep the handle clean and smooth.

Jig saw puzzle

Things to buy

One print, photograph or drawing
One piece of 4mm birch plywood the same size as the print
Contact adhesive

Tools needed

Fretsaw
Vice
Pencil
Fine glasspaper

Project: Making a jig saw puzzle

First glue the print or photograph to the plywood. Spread a thin, even layer of contact adhesive to both surfaces and allow to become touch-dry before gluing together. Bring the back of the print into contact with the plywood very carefully, starting at one edge and slowly smoothing it down as you go along, gradually letting the other edge down. Smooth down any air pockets with your fist, pushing them towards the edges.

Draw the shapes of the pieces of the puzzle on the print or photograph and, holding it on a holder clamped in a vice, cut out all the pieces. Afterwards use fine glasspaper to take away any rough edges. See page 72 for instructions on making a wooden box to hold the puzzle.

RIGHT: *This simple plywood construction is extremely useful for steadying your work when you use a coping saw. It also enables you to saw at a comfortable height, whereby the bench top and vice will not interfere with the movement of the saw frame.*

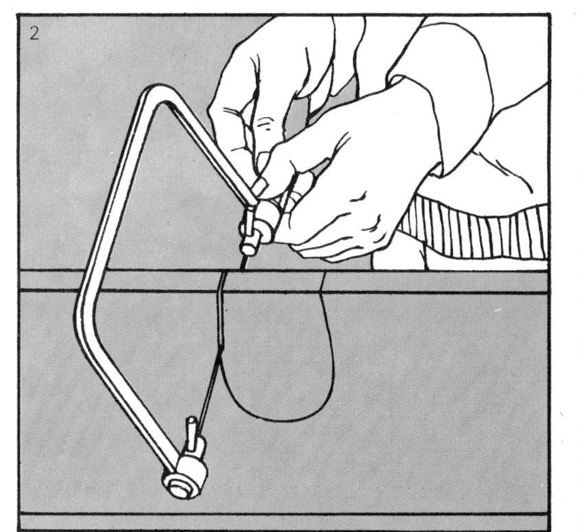

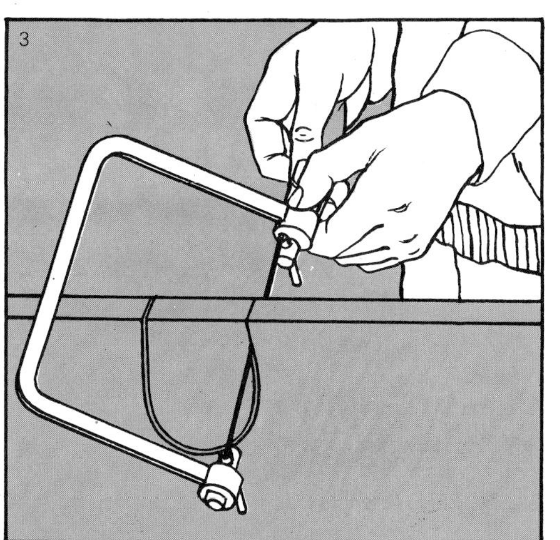

1 *To change the blade in a coping or fret saw, simply loosen the handle a few turns, slip the new blade in position and tighten up the handle.*
2 *To saw on the down stroke with a coping or fret saw, turn the blade so that the teeth face downwards.*
3 *Alternatively, install the saw blade with the teeth facing upwards for sawing on the up stroke.*

BELOW: *Provided you use a jigsaw and the purpose-built holding device fixed into the vice, it is quite easy to cut intricate shapes such as a jigsaw puzzle.*

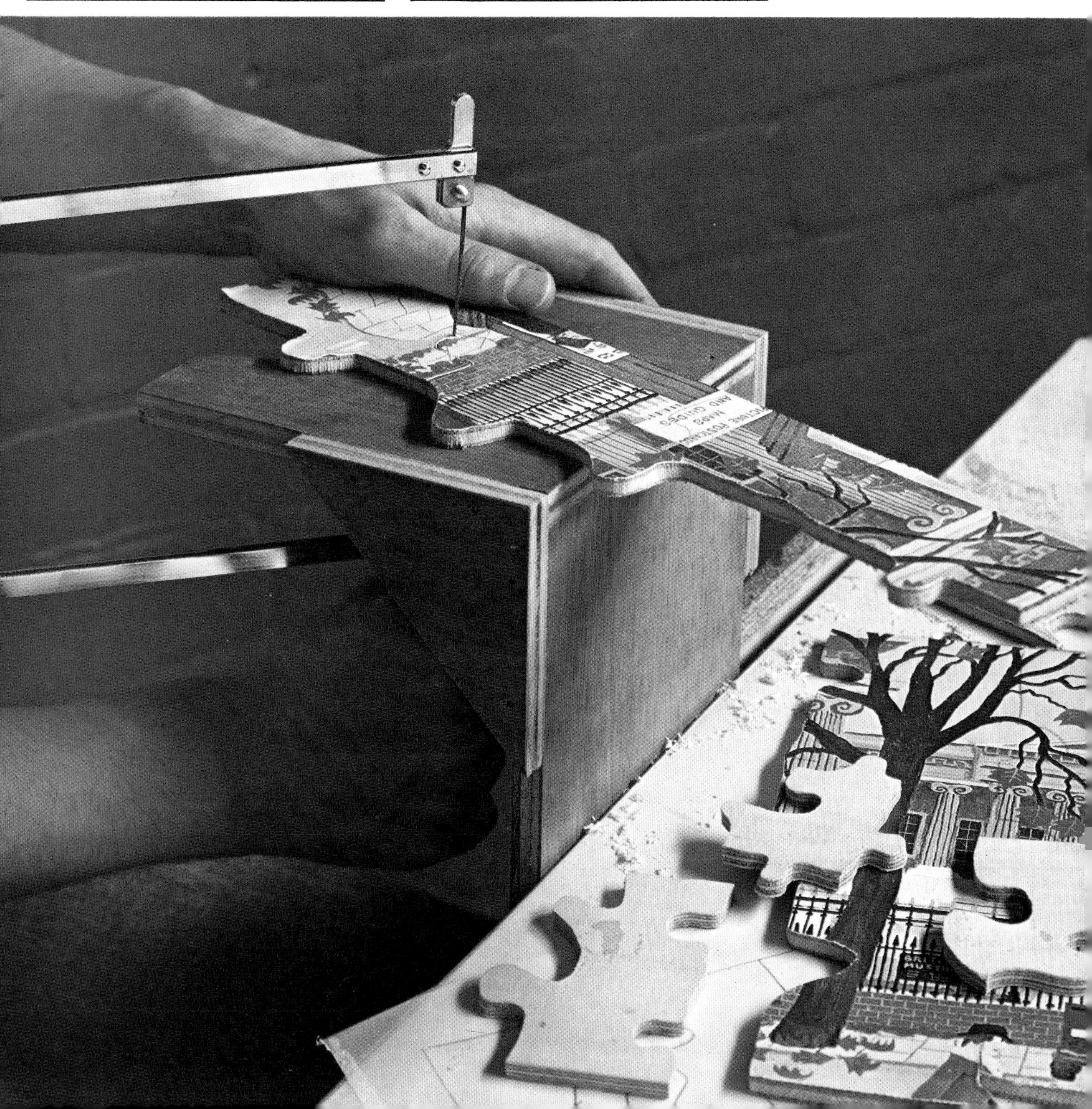

Chisels

The many types of chisels include bevel edge chisels, firmer chisels and mortise chisels. The most common is the bevel edge chisel, which has tapered sides to enable it to cut into tight corners. As with all tools, chisels are safer and more effective if they are kept very sharp. Woodworkers keep a sharpening stone on the side of the bench and sharpen their chisels periodically to keep the edge razor sharp.

Chisels come in various blade widths from 4mm to about 38mm. It is useful to have a selection of widths to choose the exact size for the job. The most useful all-purpose sizes are 6.5mm, 12mm and 19mm.

Using chisels

Chisels are used primarily to cut out wood joints, such as halving joints, but they are also used for many other small jobs such as removing wood to fit hinges and other hardware.

A chisel can be used to shave, chop, or pare the wood. It is a sharp, dangerous instrument and must be handled carefully and thoughtfully. Always hold the work down firmly in a vice and *never* hold your other hand behind the blade.

For horizontal shaving, as in cutting a halving joint, remove the wood gradually **(1)** to an exact marked depth. Make several saw cuts if possible to make it easier to remove the wood with the chisel and slice the wood away at an angle **(2)**, pushing with one hand and controlling the chisel with the other and taking off a little at a time. Work down to the mark, then work from the other side to the line and finally shave away the rest until it is smooth **(3)**.

To cut a rectangular slot such as for a mortise and tenon joint, first drill away most of the wood within the marks then use the correct width chisel with a mallet to chop away most of the wood. Remove the last layers of waste by paring with hand pressure.

Sharpening chisels

Chisels need frequent sharpening to keep them razor sharp. If the blade is badly dented or worn, it must first be ground smooth on a grinding wheel before sharpening, but usually only the edge requires sharpening on an oilstone. Spread a fine film of oil or paraffin on the stone before using it. To make sharpening easier, hold the chisel in a honing guide at the exact 30° angle (or the recommended grinding angle) rubbing it back and forth. Finally rub the flat side sideways on the stone to remove the "burr" formed in sharpening, and test the blade for sharpness.

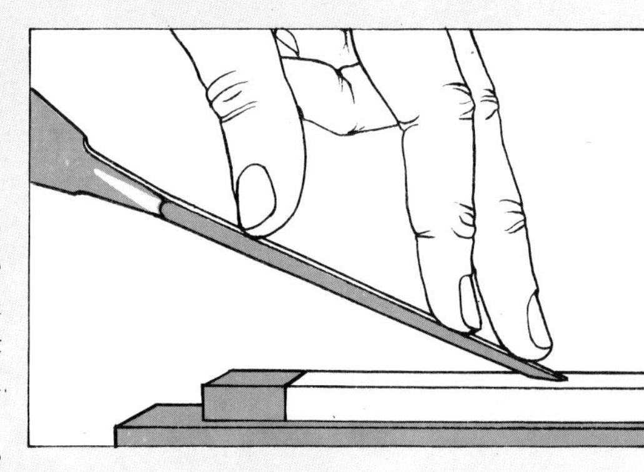

LEFT: *To sharpen the blade of a chisel, hold it at approximately 30° as shown and press down firmly as you rub it back and forth across an oiled stone.*

RIGHT: *The photograph shows the finished oilstone box made up of two identical boxes, one for the lid and one for the base. Two extra end pieces are used to hold the stone in position.*

BELOW: *Making a horizontal cut.* **1** *Cut away the wood between the marked lines from one side of the board.* **2** *Then cut to the required depth from the other side so that the waste wood forms a triangular mound.* **3** *Chisel away the waste wood, making the channel smooth.*

1

2

3

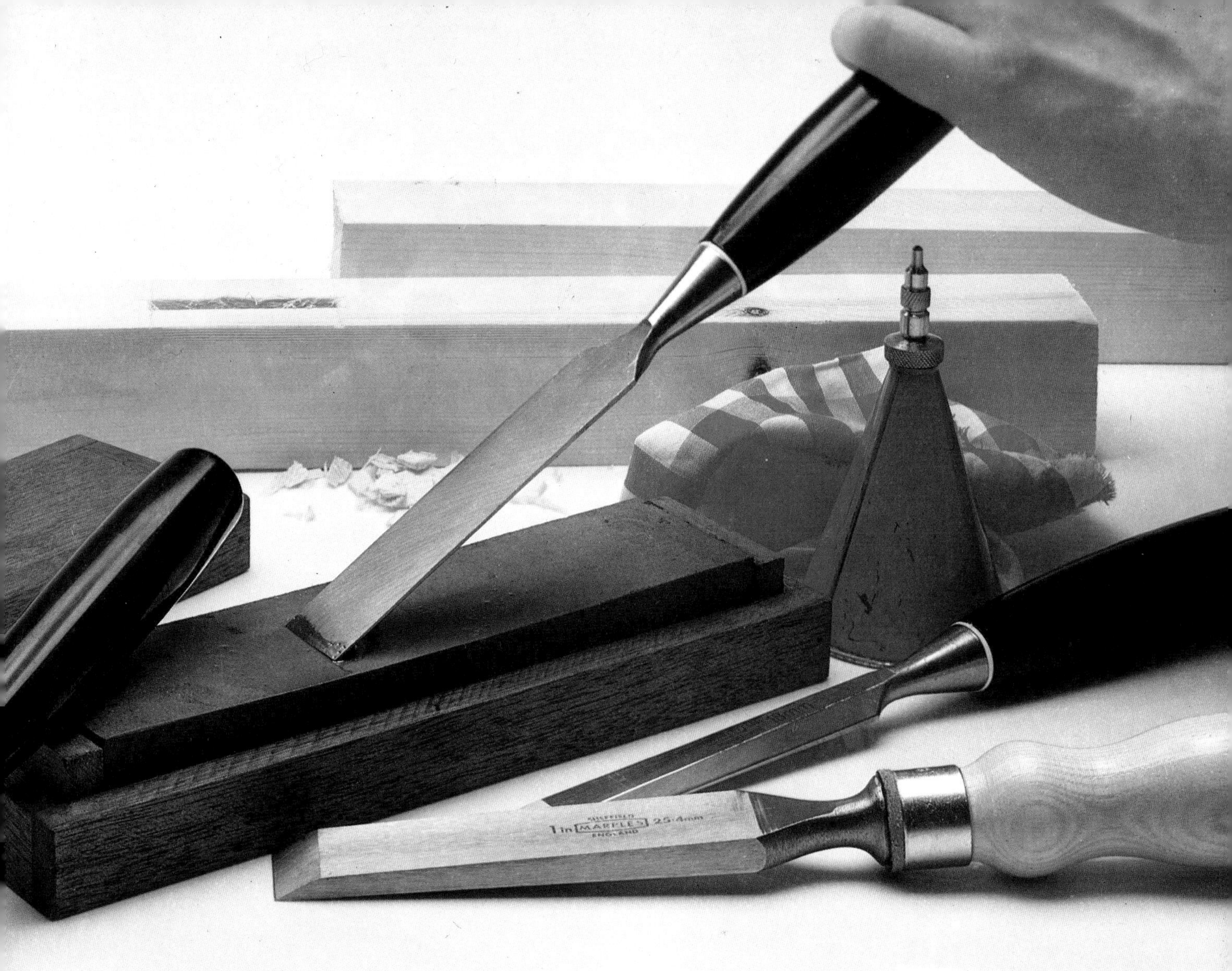

Project: Making a box for an oilstone

Cut the hardwood into the following sizes:
52mm wide: 2 pieces 224mm long (A)
23mm wide: 4 pieces 244mm long (B)
6 pieces 52mm long (C)

Glue and pin the pieces together to make two boxes as shown. Cramp the boxes up while the glue is setting. Place the oilstone in one of the boxes, with two wooden end pieces (C) to hold it in place and use the other box as a cover. If possible bevel or round the edges to give the box a more finished look.

Things to buy

- Planed hardwood such as oak or mahogany, 10mm thick, one piece 52mm wide, 460mm long
- One piece 23mm wide, approximately 1.4m long, to be cut into exact lengths
- Woodworking glue
- Approximately 30 panel pins, 90mm long

Tools required

- Tenon saw, bench hook
- Try-square
- Pin hammer, nail punch
- Pencil

Planes

Most planes are used to shave off a thin layer of wood from a board to make it straight and square. Planes are made in various lengths, sizes and shapes, from the long 600mm jointer plane to the small block plane. There are also special-purpose planes such as rebate planes, moulding planes, and compass planes which plane curved shapes.

For most practical purposes only two or three planes are required. You will need one medium length plane for straightening wood. This can be the small smoothing plane which is 200-250mm long, or the 350mm long jack plane.

Using a plane

Hold the wood firmly in place on the bench with a bench stop at the front end, and use the plane to remove any high points or slight curves in the wood. Adjust the blade iron to the required depth, then, using a long smooth motion, plane from one end right to the other, carrying through beyond the board at the end. Even shavings come with practice, but it will not take you long to enjoy the feeling of planing off long ribbon-like shavings. Check the board frequently by sighting along its length and by holding a try-square to the edge to check that it is square.

It is important to keep the plane blades (irons) sharp by frequent sharpening. Adjust the blade so that it is straight and set to the right depth to produce shavings that are the right thickness and not planing off too much at once.

Block planes The small block plane is useful for small planing jobs and because the blade is set at a low angle, for planing across end grain. Use the block plane to trim off the ends of sawn boards. Plane from both ends towards the middle to avoid splitting the wood on the corners.

Rebate planes The rebate plane is used to cut a small recess, or rebate, in framework to hold a glass or wood panel. It has an adjustable depth stop and an adjustable side fence for cutting rebates of various depths and widths. To plane a rebate, hold the plane firmly against the wood and start planing at the forward end gradually removing more and more wood further back until the entire rebate is cut.

Sharpening blades

Sharpen plane blades frequently on an oilstone as for chisel blades, holding them at an angle of 30°. Use a honing guide, if necessary, to hold the blade accurately as you rub it back and forth. Finally rub the flat backside sideways to remove the burr that has formed.

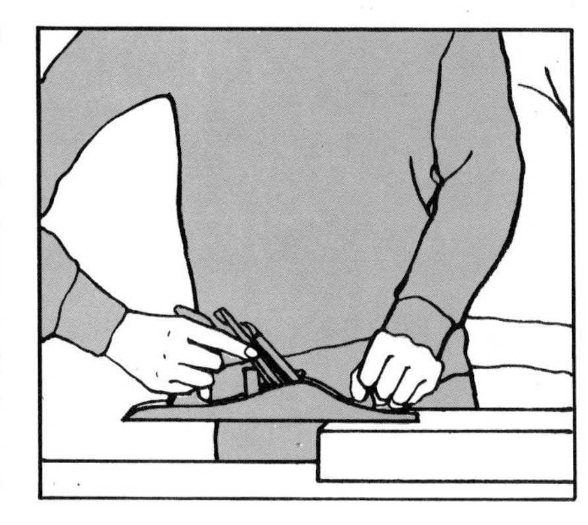

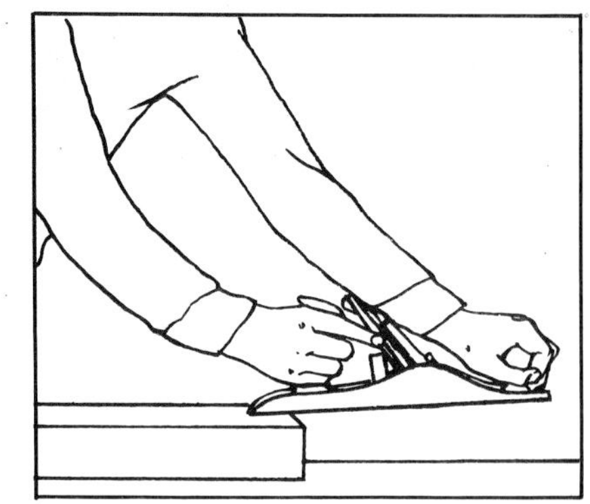

ABOVE: *The correct way to use a plane is to stand with your weight over the work, holding the plane at the edge of the board. Use a firm, sweeping motion to bring the plane across the length of the board, pressing firmly and evenly as you do so. When you reach the end of the board, continue the motion beyond it to avoid a jagged effect.*

BELOW: *An assortment of block planes and one rebate plane.*

STANLEY

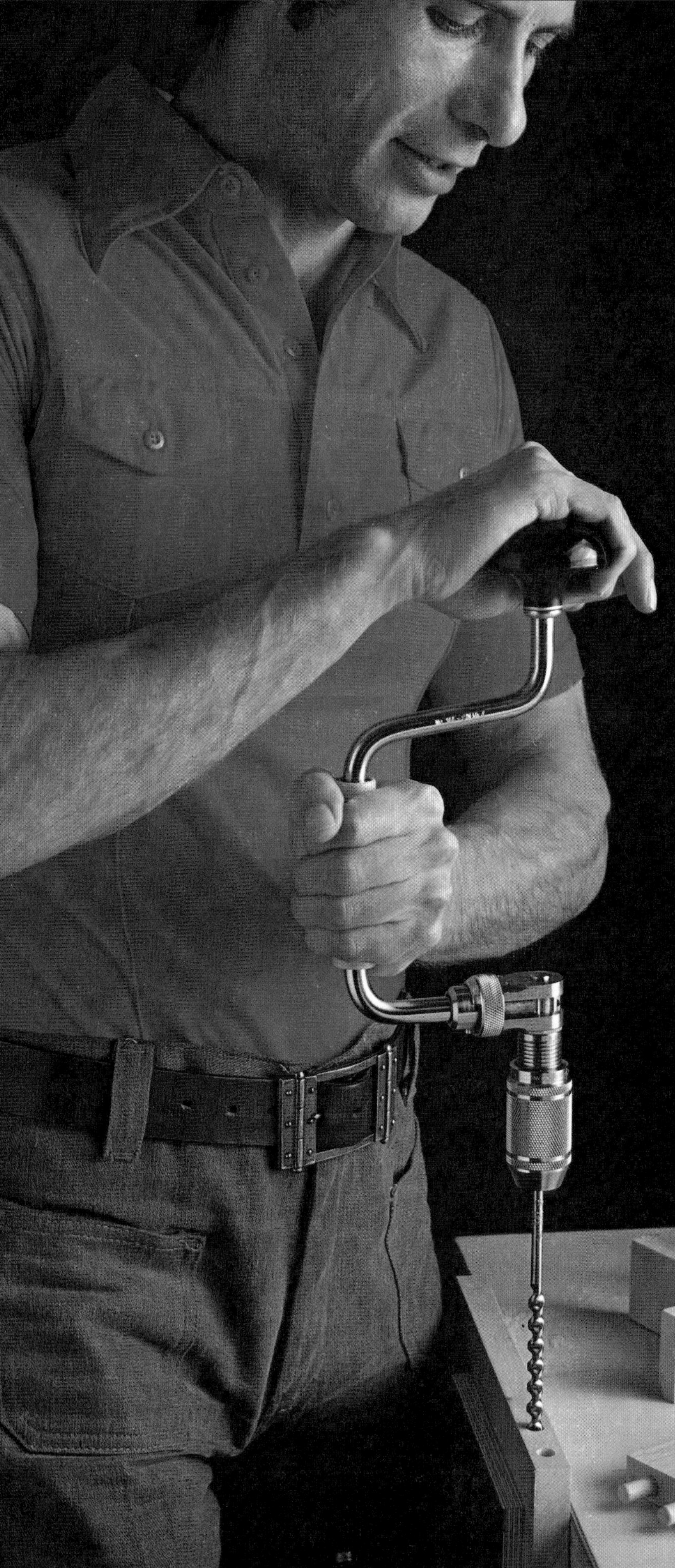

Drills

Two types of drills are used to make holes: the hand-drill and the brace. An electric drill is more versatile for most purposes but many woodworkers prefer to use hand tools.

The hand-drill Use the hand drill for small holes up to 6 or 7mm diameter, using twist drill bits. Buy a set of drill bits from approximately 1mm to 6.5mm diameter. Place the bit in the centre of the chuck and tighten it by turning the chuck with one hand while holding the handle still with the other hand.

Always punch a small hole with a centre punch or a sharpened nail, as a guide for starting the drill bit.

To drill a hole, hold the main handle with one hand and turn the handle with the other, reversing the direction to remove the drill bit. To countersink screw holes use a special countersink bit with the hand drill.

The brace Use a brace for larger and deeper holes, with auger bits for general purpose drilling or dowel drill bits for boring accurate clean holes for dowel joints (see page 63).

Auger bits are available in sizes from 6.5mm to about 38mm diameter, but the most useful sizes are 9mm, 12mm, 19mm and 25mm diameters. You can also buy a countersink bit and even a screwdriver bit for use in the brace. The screwdriver bit is particularly handy for large jobs. Fasten the bits in the chuck of the brace by holding the chuck firmly as you turn the handle.

To use the brace, put pressure with one hand

LEFT AND FAR RIGHT: *When using either a brace or a hand drill, hold it vertically to the surface before you turn the handle. Use one hand to steady the drill and the other hand to turn it, as shown.*

on the formed head as you turn the handle with the other. Drill slowly, particularly in hardwoods, and check that you are holding the drill vertically by placing a try-square on the bench near the work. Never drill straight through a piece of wood. To avoid splitting the underside, drill until just the point of the drill bit shows through, then turn the wood over and finish the hole from the other side.

To drill holes to a fixed depth use a depth stop. For most work it is enough to stick a piece of tape around the bit at the correct depth. For more accurate work make a simple depth stop.

Making a depth stop Carefully drill a hole in a piece of 38 × 38mm offcut using the required size drill bit. It may be necessary to clamp both sides to avoid splitting the wood. Cut off the depth stop to the required length, shape the end to a taper and slide it on the drill bit so that the required length of drill bit protrudes.

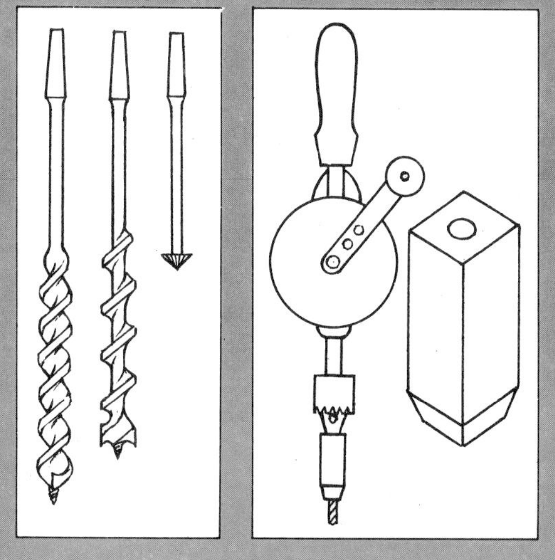

ABOVE, FROM LEFT: *Auger, dowel and countersink bits; each can be used in a brace. A depth stop is a useful attachment for obtaining accurate results, with each hole drilled to the same depth.*

Screwdrivers

Screwdrivers have tips of varying sizes and it is important to use the correct screwdriver to fit each screw. The wrong size screwdriver often results in damaged wood around the screw or in a ruined screwhead.

Use the standard straight slot screwdriver for ordinary slotted screws and the Phillips screwdriver for cross slotted screws. It is useful to have three or four screwdrivers of varying types and sizes.

Ratchet screwdrivers A ratchet screwdriver allows you to turn the screw without changing your grip. The most convenient type is the pump action ratchet, commonly known as the Yankee screwdriver. With this type the various sizes of blades are interchangeable and one screwdriver can be used for all screws. It can also be used in a pump action, just pushing down on the handle to turn in the screw quickly. It can be quite a dangerous tool; it often pinches the fingers or slips off the screwhead and damages the wood. It is a convenient tool but must be used carefully and with respect. When not in use, store it in a dry place.

Shaping and finishing tools

Rasps, files and surforms are very useful for shaping wood into irregular forms or for rounding corners and edges.

Rasps are used only on wood. They are available in various sizes and grades of teeth. Buy a 250mm long general purpose rasp with a half-round shape on the back side. Use it for scraping rough shapes in wood held in a vice with one hand firmly on the handle and the other pressing the abrasive rasp into the wood.

Surforms are a convenient modern substitute for rasps. They come in various easy-to-hold sizes and shapes and have replaceable blades. Use the surforms with a pushing or pulling action, depending on the type, to shape the wood. Surforms are specially useful for making sculptures or models in wood.

Finish off the rough surface left by a rasp or surform with a file. Buy a file with one side slightly coarser than the other; use the rough side first and finish off with the smooth side. The same files are also used in metalwork.

Sanding blocks To smooth down a rough surface in preparation for the final finish (see page 85) use glasspaper or garnet paper wrapped around a cork sanding block. Tear the glasspaper into quarters against the edge of the bench and wrap the piece around the sanding block, which will keep it flat as you sand the wood. If you hold the paper directly in your hand it tends to cause hollows in the surface as you sand.

Cabinet scrapers Scrapers are thin pieces of flat steel which are used by cabinet makers to shave off very thin layers of wood to make the surface satin smooth. Scrapers are used successfully only on hardwoods and produce a much finer and smoother surface than sanding, which tends to clog the grain with dust.

Scrapers should be carefully sharpened with a fine file, oilstone and burnisher to create a very sharp edge. The scraper does not scrape the wood but shaves away a thin layer of wood.

A useful alternative for the amateur woodworker is the scraper plane which does the same job but is easier to use. It has a blade like a plane mounted between two handles to make it easier to push it forward.

Cramps

Cramps and vices are used for several woodworking jobs.
THIS PAGE: *Three G-cramps and one sash cramp.* OPPOSITE: *A mitre cramp on its own and in use tightening a picture frame, and a vice.*

Cramps are indispensable for woodworking. Even the smallest job needs to be held down to a worktop, and without a vice, a G-cramp is the easiest way to do it.

There are several types of cramps but the most useful are the G-cramp for small to medium jobs, the mitre cramp for holding frame corners together, and the sash-cramp for gluing up several boards into table or counter tops.

Cramps are quite expensive and there never seem to be enough of them in the woodworker's kit, but there are many simple cramping devices you can make yourself, which will serve as inexpensive substitutes.

G-cramps The two pieces of, say, a halving joint must be held firmly together until the glue sets. Occasionally, nails or screws are good enough to hold them, but more often a G-cramp will do it better. Spread a thin layer of glue on one of the pieces and bring the joint together, cramping firmly.

G-cramps come in sizes from 50mm to 200mm, and the right size must be chosen for the job, although the 150mm size is convenient for most work. Always use small pieces of wood, cardboard or rubber under the jaws of the cramp to protect the wood underneath. Even the lightest pressure tends to leave small indentations which are difficult to remove, so always remember this precaution.

Cramp the pieces together with light pressure. Cramping too tightly forces the glue out of the joint. For larger joints use two or perhaps three G-cramps to provide even pressure. Leave the work cramped up until the glue has set. White PVA woodworking glue sets in about 30 minutes which is fast and convenient, as you will probably need the cramps for the next joint.

Mitre cramps Mitre cramps hold the mitred pieces of a frame absolutely square until the glue has set. They are normally used in sets of four, one for each corner to glue the whole frame at once. They are quite expensive but it is easy to make a simple home-made substitute from four corner blocks and a piece of heavy cord, tightened with a stick or short length of dowel. This is a very quick and effective way of making picture frames. (See page 68 for instructions on cutting and assembling a simple picture frame.)

Sash cramps A table top or any large surface made from solid wood will need several boards glued together to make up the necessary width. Today most tops are made by applying veneers to a piece of chipboard, which is a much simpler process as the sheet is large, stable and flat. Veneered tops do not compare well in durability and lasting beauty with solid wood. Working with beautiful woods is worth planing the boards straight and gluing them to get a solid top.

To cramp up long boards you will need

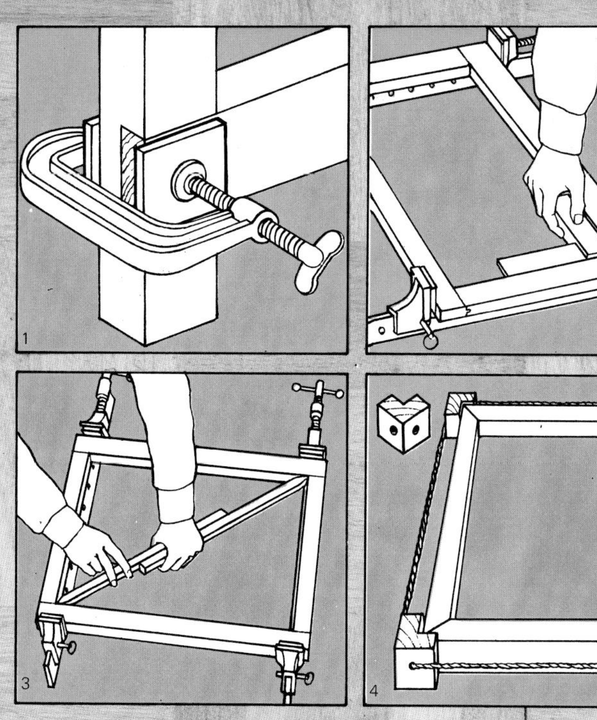

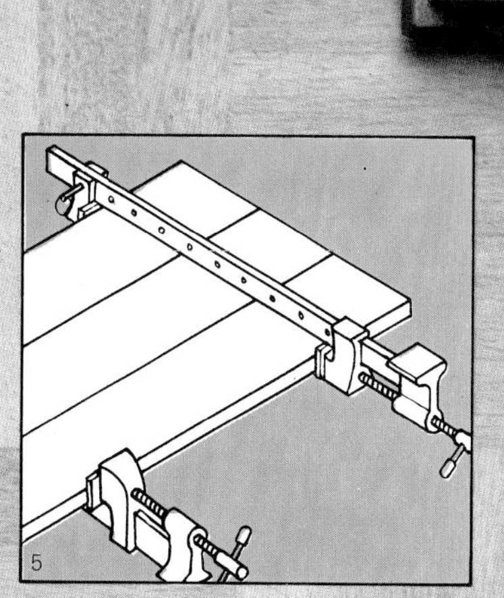

several sash cramps, one about 100-150mm in from either end and a few in between. Alternate the cramps under and over the wood otherwise the boards tend to bow. Remember to use pieces of scrap wood under the heads to prevent marking the wood.

In gluing up, say, a dowelled frame, make sure the framework is square as you tighten the cramps. Always lay the work on a sturdy level surface, and check the corners with a try-square as you go along. A convenient way to check is to measure the diagonals with two sticks sharpened to a point.

When the diagonals are equal the frame is square. It may be necessary to place the cramps slightly skew to correct a distorted frame.

Sash cramps are very expensive to buy. A less expensive alternative is to buy separate cramp heads which are mounted on a piece of sturdy wood the right length to suit the job. Alternatively make up your own clamping devices with a few offcuts screwed directly to a bench or a piece of heavy plywood.

Screw two parallel boards down with stout No. 10 screws and plane up two pairs of hardwood wedges about 200mm long. Place the glued frame between the boards and tap the wedges together with a hammer to tighten it. This is a simple, effective solution to an expensive problem, and works equally well for gluing up large tops, although these will require further pairs of wedges.

Vices

A good woodworking vice will hold wood firmly, leaving your hands free to saw, chisel, mark or drill. As with all other tools, the best vice to buy is the most expensive you can afford. The vice on the workbench on page 49 is attached with four coachbolts. It is very strong, will grip large pieces of wood, and has a quick release mechanism which allows you to close or open the vice without turning the screw handle.

For occasional small projects you can use a small vice which clamps onto a table top or to a temporary work surface. It does not have the strength of a permanent bench vice, but it will serve perfectly well for most of the projects in this book.

DIAGRAMS, ABOVE: **1** *A G-cramp padded with waste wood to protect the work holds the pieces of a halving joint in place while the glue sets.* **2** *Sash cramps hold the corners of this dowelled frame together while the joints set. Use a try-square to ensure the assembly is square.* **3** *A good alternative method of checking the corners is to measure the diagonals to see that they are equal.* **4** *To make your own mitre cramps use small blocks of wood, as shown, at each corner and draw string through each and around the whole work to hold it all together.* **5** *Sash cramps are used to hold large glued surfaces.*

Power tools

BOTTOM RIGHT: *To remove or install a drill bit, turn the chuck clockwise with the special key that comes with the drill, holding the body of the tool firmly in the other hand.*

OPPOSITE: *A vertical drill stand allows you to drill holes perfectly vertical and to a precise depth. It is a very welcome device for repetitious drilling and would be a useful aid for making the holes in the shelving system shown on page 65.*

Most professional woodworkers do not use hand tools such as drills and saws when a power tool will do the job much quicker and often more accurately. Larger workshops and factories, of course, cut, drill and shape the wood using large and very expensive machinery which does the job almost automatically.

The most common power tools used by the home woodworkers are the drill, circular saw, jig saw and sander. The versatile drill is a virtual necessity; it can drill holes in wood, metal, and even glass. Drill attachments convert the drill into a sander, circular saw, jig saw, or even a small lathe.

A circular saw, jig saw, and sander are very convenient for the busy woodworker, particularly for cutting large sheets of plywood or chipboard, and often produce a faster, more accurate job than the equivalent hand tools.

Using power tools safely

All power tools are dangerous if they are not used carefully. Professional woodworkers treat power tools with a great deal of respect and form good working habits so that safety becomes almost second nature to them. It is most important not to worry or hurry when using a power tool. Uncertainty and hesitation cause accidents. Read the manufacturer's instructions carefully before using the tool. Use all machines respectfully and carefully, but with confidence.

Before using any electrical tool, first check the wiring and replace any cut or frayed wire immediately. Check the plug frequently. Always unswitch and, for added safety, remove the plug from the socket when working on the tool or when changing the blade. When working with a power tool the flex tends to get in the way. The best solution is to use a fairly long flex and pass it over your shoulder. This is particularly important when cutting with the circular saw. Another important safety point is never to wear loose clothing or have a tie dangling. Roll up sleeves and tie up long hair to prevent it getting caught in the machine. Make it a habit to check all these safety points when you use the tools.

Use the tools with a moderate amount of pressure. Drill bits and saw blades become dull with use, and if too much pressure is needed it may be necessary to resharpen them. If the tools are not sharp enough, the blades will cause burns in the wood and may even wear out the motors

Accurate cutting and drilling requires practice. Power tools feel strange when you start to use them, but you will soon become accustomed to them and find it difficult to revert to laborious manual tasks which take a few seconds to do by machine.

Power drill

The power drill is relatively inexpensive to buy and quite safe to use. The two speed model is a good investment. The fast speed is used to drill wood, and the slower speed is for drilling metal and masonry to hang up shelves on to a brick wall, for example. Buy a drill which also has a hammer action for faster drilling into masonry. For general woodworking only, a simple fast speed drill is good enough.

The main features of the drill are the handle and trigger, which turns the power on and off, the body, containing the motor, and the chuck, which holds the drill bits securely. On variable speed models there is also a speed change switch, and a switch to turn on the hammer action if it has this feature.

Drill bits For general drilling use ordinary twist drills available singly by diameter or in mixed-sized sets up to a diameter of 12mm. Twist drills are designed for metalwork only but they are widely used in woodworking to drill clearance and pilot holes for wood screws. For faster, cleaner holes in making dowel joints, for example, use special machine auger bits or dowel bits. The most useful drill bits for drilling large holes are the flat bits ranging from 6.5mm up to about 38mm in diameter. Flat bits are used only in power drills. The larger sizes can be dangerous to use, particularly if the drill is hand held. The drill should be mounted in a drill stand to keep it stable when drilling large holes with flat bits.

To mount the bit in the drill, unplug the drill and turn the chuck by hand to enlarge the opening. Insert the bit, tighten the chuck by hand to hold the bit in place, and finish tightening with the chuck key.

Practise drilling holes that are straight and square with the wood. It is quite difficult to judge whether you are holding the drill vertically: stand a try-square on the workbench next to the drill to guide you, or get another person to tell you whether the drill is vertical.

Most drill bits can be sharpened with special tools and devices available at hardware shops.

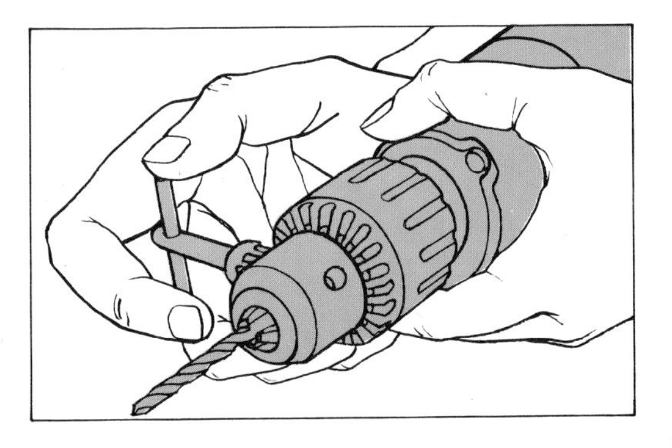

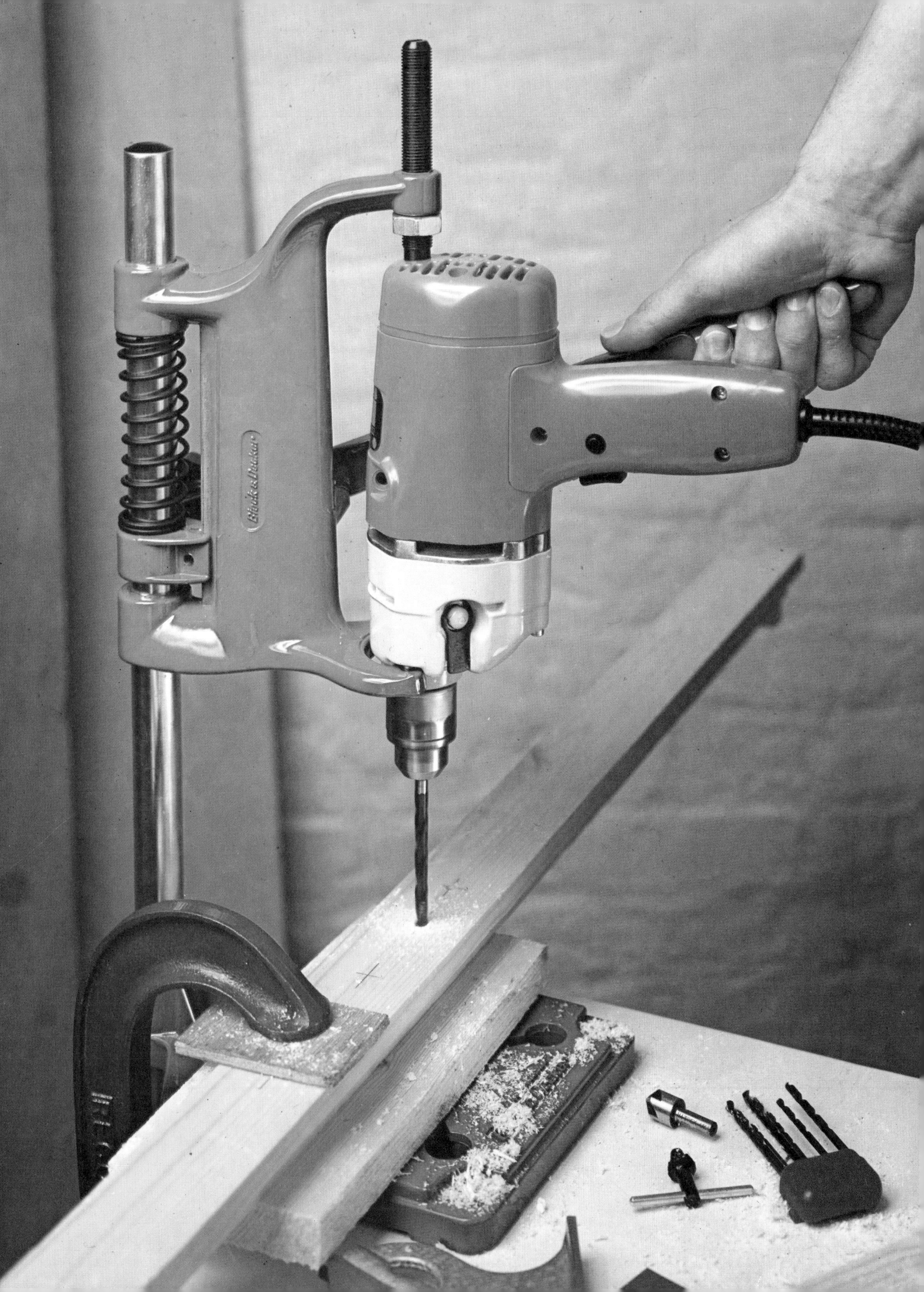

Attachments for the drill

A drill stand is invaluable for drilling accurate vertical holes to exact depths. Most drill manufacturers sell stands for use with their drills. Mount the drill firmly and cramp the work being drilled to the bench below if necessary and use the handle to lower the drill into the work. The drill stand has a depth adjustment; to drill a series of holes to exactly the same depth you simply set the depth, test it on an offcut and then drill the holes one after the other.

You can also buy a horizontal stand to mount the drill for use with wire brushes, sanding discs and even a grinding wheel attachment.

See manufacturer's catalogue for the accessories available for the basic power drill. The most useful ones are the circular saw and the sanding attachments.

Circular saw attachment

For cutting thin plywood up to about 12mm thickness and for cutting small softwood and hardwood sections, use the circular saw attachment for the drill. It takes time to convert the drill to a saw and if you need a circular saw often it may be better to buy an integral circular saw, described on page 39.

The saw blades of the circular saw attachment are either 125 or 150mm in diameter, giving a depth of cut between 38 and 45mm, but in practice the cut is limited by the power of the drill motor and you will soon learn by experience what kind of cuts your saw attachment can make.

Follow the manufacturer's instructions when assembling the saw attachment, and use it with great care. Read the safety instructions on page 40 and follow them carefully. When used safely the circular saw attachment is a very versatile and convenient way of getting more use from your drill.

Use it exactly as you would an integral circular saw. See page 39 for full instructions.

Sanding attachments

For rough sanding such as stripping paint off old furniture, a flexible disc attachment is very useful. A circular disc of glasspaper is mounted on to a rubber pad or a circular disc and the tool is then used either free hand or as a rigid bench sander on a horizontal stand.

For fine sanding in preparation for applying a finish, use an orbital sanding attachment. Begin with a medium coarse paper, and progress to very fine glasspaper for a really smooth finish. For even better results buy an inexpensive integral sander like the one shown on page 41.

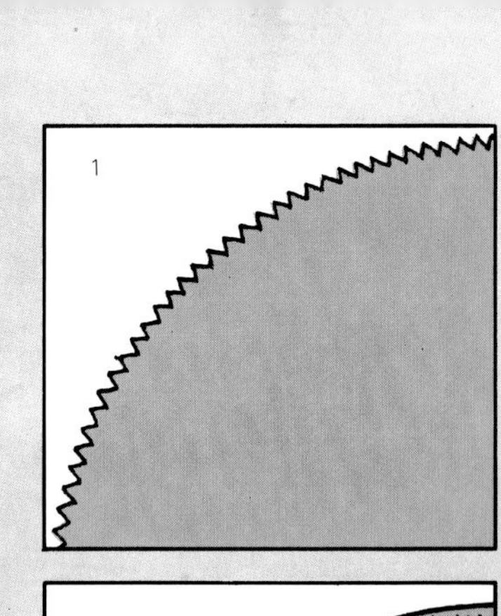

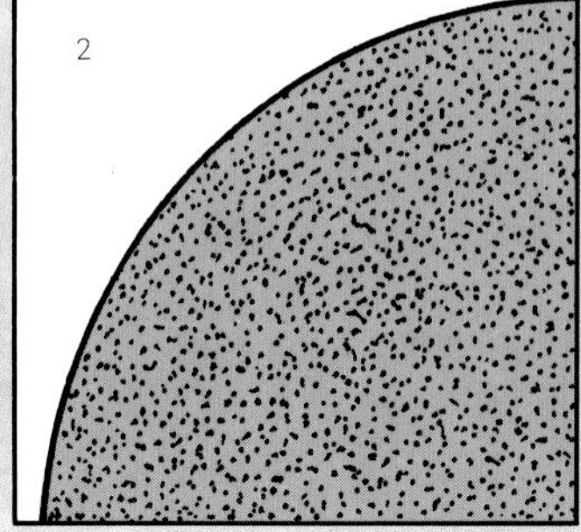

ABOVE AND RIGHT: *Circular saw blades.* **1** *Crosscut blade for smooth cuts across the grain.* **2** *Abrasive blade for slate, plastics, tiles and masonry.* **3** *Rip blade for rough cutting with the grain.* **4** *Combination blade for ripping and crosscutting.* **5** *Carbide-tipped blade for timber or harder materials.*

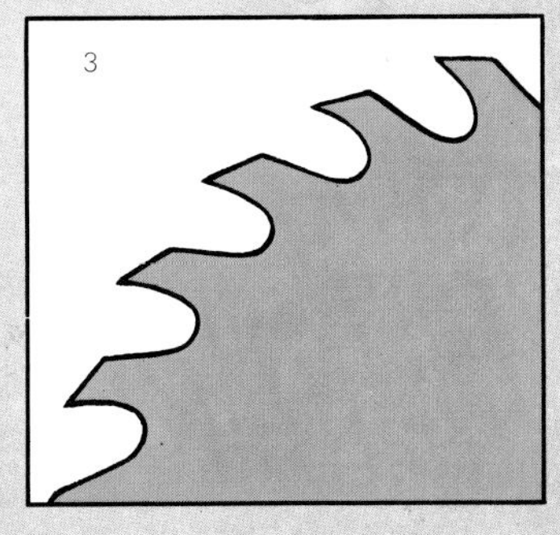

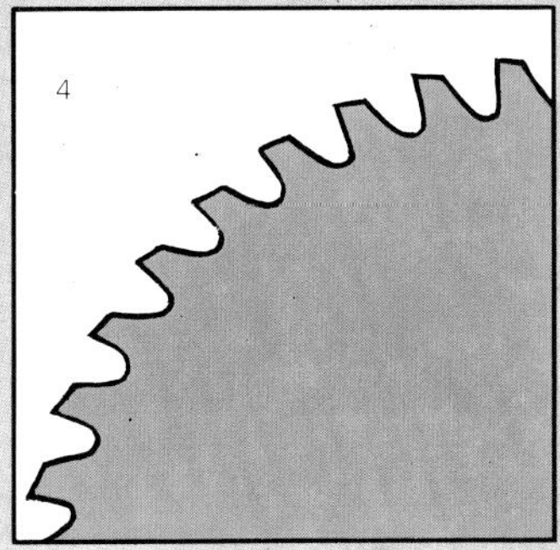

Other power tools

Circular saw

The integral circular saw is in constant use in any woodworking shop. Small saws are available to take 125mm diameter blades, but for more general use such as cutting up thick sheets of plywood buy one to take 188mm blades. There are several types of blade for various jobs. The rough rip blade cuts with the grain, the finer crosscut saw cuts across the grain, but the best blade is the combination blade which will do both ripping and crosscutting.

For the very best results buy a more expensive carbide tipped blade which is longer lasting and cuts cleanly through almost all materials.

The circular saw can be a very dangerous tool if not used properly. Follow the safety instructions on page 40 and make a habit of using the saw carefully, without rushing the work. Always hold it firmly and do not let go of the tool if the blade should grab the wood and kick the saw. A little practice will give you confidence in sawing at the right speed.

The saw is fitted with a spring guard which automatically covers the blade as you pull it away from the wood.

For most jobs you can saw without a fence, guiding the saw along the line using the small notch in the sole plate. First set the depth of cut to saw all the way through the wood or perhaps part of the way for making grooves. Hold the handle firmly with one hand and the body of the saw with the other. Concentrate on the sawing and if interrupted, do not look up before shutting the saw off.

To make long cuts in timber or plywood parallel to the edge use the rip fence which comes with the saw or for the best results, particularly in cutting up large sheets, clamp a straight edge to the work and use it to guide the saw along. Notice that the guide must be set a distance away from the cut. Determine the exact distance by trying it on an offcut and write the measurement on the straight edge for future reference. The saw blade removes 2 to 4mm of wood, so make sure to cut on the waste side of the line to end up with the exact size measured to the line.

Keep the saw clean and have it maintained regularly and repaired by the manufacturer. The saw blades will need periodic sharpening or they will cut unevenly or burn the wood. Take them to a large hardware shop who will have it done for you.

To change blades, make sure that the teeth face in the right direction, indicated by the arrow on the blade. First shut off the power then tighten the nut and washer with the spanner provided with the saw.

Jig saw

In many ways jig saws are the most versatile of all power saws. A jig saw is much easier and safer to use than a circular saw. The blade works with an up and down action, cutting on the up stroke. Although it is intended mainly to cut circles and irregular shapes in wood, it can also be used to make crosscuts and short ripcuts in wood, plywood and chipboard. There are many types of blades, from the very fine toothed blades for cutting metal to the coarser blades used in rough cutting of wood. Buy a good quality, robust jig saw with enough power to cut through at least 19mm plywood. It is extremely frustrating, when using a cheap saw, when the blade drifts or slants when cutting through heavy material. The high cost of plywood justifies the more expensive model.

The method for holding the blade in place varies from model to model, but it is usually tightened by means of a special Allen key which comes with the saw. Blade-changing is very quick and you should keep a few of each kind on hand and change to the right one for each job.

Most sawing with the jig saw is done by following a curve by eye. Hold the handle firmly and go only as fast through the wood as the saw will let you. If the blade causes smoking or burning you are trying to saw too fast or the blade is dull. The blades are disposable, so throw away the dull one and insert a sharp one.

Although it is a safer tool to use than the circular saw, the jig saw is still a dangerous tool and must be treated with respect. The most common accidents result from cutting through the cord. Hang the lead over your shoulder as you work to keep it away from the blade. Always clamp the work to be cut, checking that the saw blade will not pass through the bench. *Never, never* reach underneath near the blade to hold the wood, as this is extremely dangerous. Make a habit of using the correct techniques and the jig saw will be a safe reliable tool.

The jig saw is not designed to cut straight lines like the circular saw, but with a wooden fence or straight edge it can make a reasonably straight cut across or along the grain. Clamp the straight edge the appropriate distance from the line to be cut and guide the saw carefully along it. Do not force the saw. If the blade starts to drift pull the saw back and gently re-cut along the correct path. The finish with a jig saw is quite rough so cut about a millimetre on the waste side of the line to allow you to clean the cut with a plane.

To make frequent crosscuts it is worth making a T-square guide out of two pieces of wood screwed and glued at an exact 90° angle. Make the front piece longer and cut it off with the jig saw, using the guide to line up the cut end with the line. Clamp the T-square on to the wood to make the cut.

A homemade T-square makes the job of jig sawing much easier. To make one, simply glue and screw together two pieces of softwood at right angles and cut off one arm of the T by running the jig saw along the guide indicated by the dotted lines in **1**. *When using the T-square, line up the cut-off end parallel with the cutting mark, shown in* **2**, *clamp it down and then run the saw along.* **3** *Clamp a straight edge firmly across the work you are cutting as a guide for the saw.*

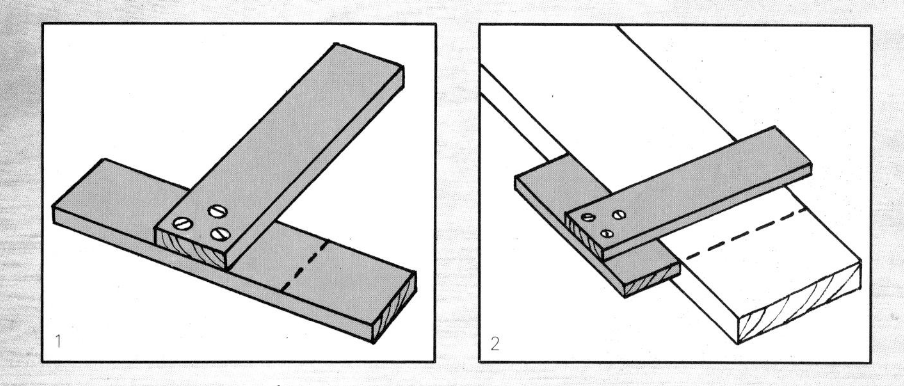

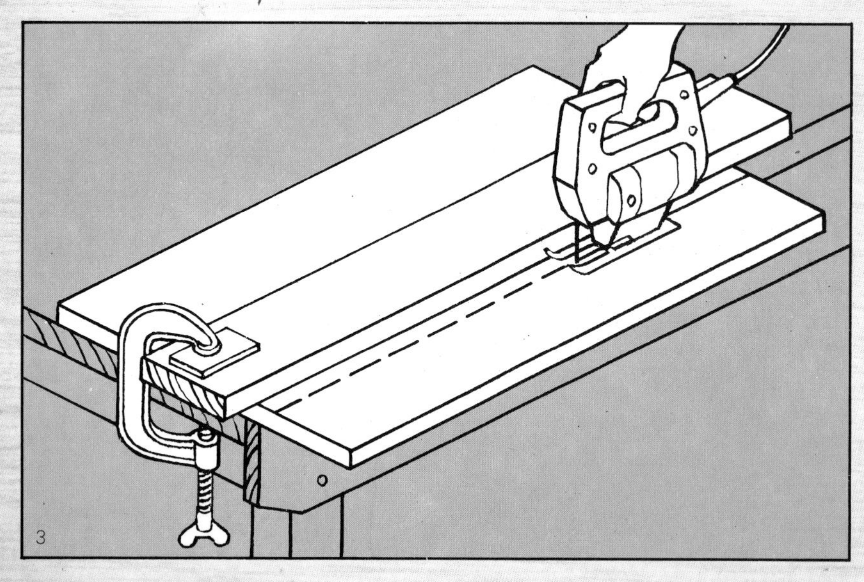

Power sander

Hand-sanding is hard work. For small, occasional jobs use a sanding block with glasspaper to smooth down the surface. For larger projects use a power sander. Very rough work requires an expensive belt sander but for most fine finishing work a small and inexpensive orbital sander is just right.

There are several types of power sander on the market. Flexible disc sanding attachments fit on to the end of the electric drill. Disc sanders are used mostly for rough work and with a special buffing attachment for bringing up polished surfaces.

Belt sanders are intended for fairly rough sanding such as taking paint off old furniture. They usually come fitted with a special dustbag which collects the sanding dust. These machines are quite difficult to control and are not recommended for fine finishing.

The best machine for furniture finishing is the orbital sander. There is a small inexpensive model which will do the work very well and a larger industrial model fitted with a dust bag.

Orbital sanders work with a fast oscillating motion, the pad constantly moving in small circles. When a coarse paper is used, however, you can often see small circular marks. These are caused by loose pieces of grit getting caught under the sandpaper, and are prevented by brushing off the surface frequently.

There are several grades of glasspaper for use in the orbital sander. It is useful to have a supply of coarse, medium and fine glasspaper. The method of changing the paper varies according to the type of sander but is quite easy on all machines.

Start sanding with coarse or medium paper, depending on the surface. Hold the sander in both hands, applying even pressure. The sander will not work any faster or better if it is pushed down hard; a light pressure gives the best results. For the final sanding use fine paper and carefully go over the entire surface, overlapping strokes as you move the sander along. The sander can be moved slowly with or across the grain, but it is a good habit to sand with the grain. For an especially fine finish it may be necessary to finish off sanding by hand with a very fine garnet paper. Remember the professional trick of wiping the surface with a slightly damp rag to raise the grain and allowing the surface to dry before the final sanding.

The portable electric router

The router has always been considered to be one of those tools which is used only by people in the trade. In fact the router is the easiest to use of all the portable power tools. It is an ideal tool for the amateur woodworker because it does a lot of otherwise very difficult jobs safely and easily.

As with other power tools such as the saw and drill, the router is basically an electric motor with cutters mounted on a shaft. But unlike drills and saws which perform only one basic function, the router can be used with a variety of cutters to do many different jobs, such as cutting grooves and rebates, shaping edges or making dovetails.

Each cutter is bought separately to do a specific job, but after a while you accumulate enough cutters to make the router very versatile. The cutters have a short shaft which is either 6.5mm or 9.5mm in diameter and which fits into a matching hole on the router. They are fastened either with a special Allen key or with a spanner provided with the router. Some large routers will take either size shaft but the small inexpensive routers will usually only take the 6.5mm shaft. When buying cutters, make sure to specify the shaft diameter.

Routers consist of the main body containing the motor, the shaft which holds the cutters and the adjustable base-plate which is moved along the wood surface as the router cuts. The base-plate can be adjusted up or down to expose more or less cutter and thus to give a deep or shallow cut. It is always best to test the cut on a piece of scrap wood to make sure the depth of cut is exactly right.

The most common uses of the router are to make grooves and to cut rebates and moulded edges on items of furniture. Keep in mind that the router relies on speed of rotation rather than on power for its cutting action and the depth of cut will therefore be limited. If, for example, you are cutting an 18mm wide groove in a piece of blockboard, it will be necessary probably to make two or three runs to get the required depth. For each run you simply adjust the depth another 3mm or so.

Once you get used to the router, you will find it the most useful tool in the workshop. You can increase its usefulness by buying or making various jigs and guides, such as a circular cutting guide or dovetail template. If you need further information, simply refer to the manufacturer's instructions.

Unlike the other portable power tools, the router is never used free hand. For most jobs such as rebating or grooving you use an adjustable fence which runs along the edge of the wood to guide the cutter parallel to the edge. But you can also run the base-plate against a straight-edge clamped onto the wood as a guide. Most moulding cutters have a built-in guide. The small extension on the base of the cutter is like a wheel which runs along the side of the wood to guide the cutter along the edge in cutting mouldings and rebates.

To use the router safely, first make sure the work is cramped down firmly, then unplug the machine while you make sure the cutter is mounted firmly and the plate and fences are adjusted correctly. When using the router, guide it along so that it cuts smoothly, fast enough not to burn the wood but not so fast that it causes the wood to split and the motor to work too hard. You'll get used to the sound of the motor and adjust your motion accordingly. Remember that the cutter, which rotates clockwise, should always cut 'into' the wood. Hold the handles firmly with both hands to make sure not to get the electric cord caught in the machine.

After finishing the cut, move the router up and away from the wood in a continuous motion, and shut off the motor, making sure it has stopped before putting the router down.

With practice you will find the router a useful tool for finishing edges, making mouldings and, when you become more advanced, for cutting dovetail joints.

RIGHT: *The router can be fitted with a guide which fits onto the base of the tool. Push the base along the edge of the work to make cuts parallel with the edge. A guide like this is essential, since the router is rarely used freehand*

For a highly professional edge to your work, the router is the tool to use – and easy to manipulate as long as the instructions are followed. There is a wide range of cutters available.

1 *The chamfer or bevel bit cuts the edge of the timber at a 45-degree angle.*
2 *The beading bit is used frequently when a decorative edge is required.*

3 *The rounding-over bit can be used to round over the edge or, as shown here, with a step-down for a mixed effect.*

4 *A core-box bit is used for cutting channels or grooves in the surface of the timber. To make you own tongued-and-grooved panelling, this would be the router to use.*

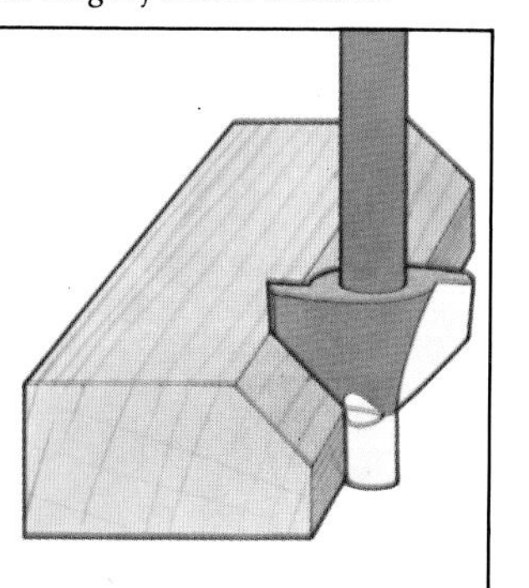

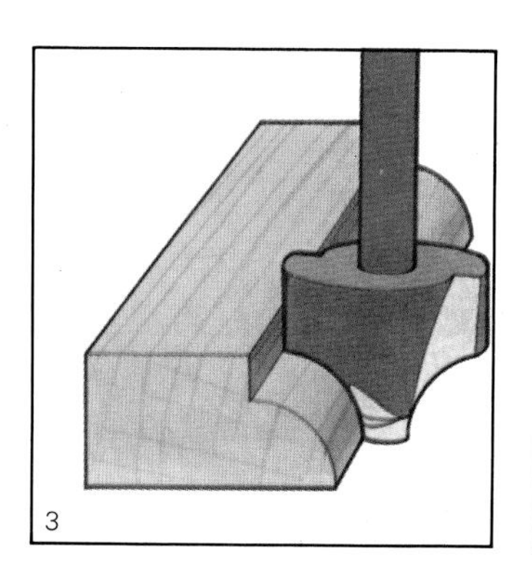

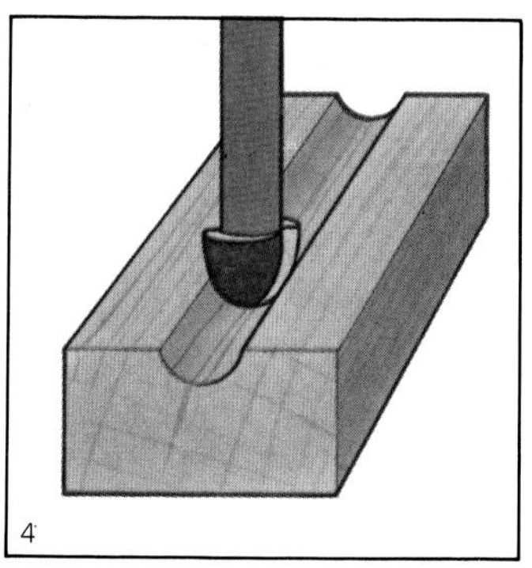

Black & Decker
16 A
360 W
30,000
1
DOUBLE
INSULATED
ROUTER
DN 65

The work area

OPPOSITE: A fold-down work table **(1)** *fixed to a batten screwed to the wall makes an excellent working bench that can be folded flat against the wall when not in use. The slatted wall rack above it is easy to make (page 47) and provides ample storage space for tools. The fold-down table legs* **(2)** *are supported by a special bracket* **(3)** *which allows the legs to be folded up when the table is not in use.* **4** *A tool box hung on the wall with hinged doors fitted to hold additional tools is a convenient place to store hand tools, hardware and small tins.* **5** *A small portable tool box made from softwood offcuts is always handy for keeping tools together and transporting them from place to place while you work.*

No work space is ever large enough. It is well known that the amount of space required for storage, work and machines is always more than the space available. The amount of space needed very often depends on people's habits. A tidy person who cleans up and hangs up the tools as he goes along can work successfully in a much smaller space than someone who waits until the job is finished before straightening up.

Your workshop area will obviously depend on the amount of available space. With more people living in flats today, space is more limited and very few of us are able to fit out a garage, garden shed or basement as a complete workshop. But no matter how limited the space, there is usually a corner in a spare room or loft that can serve as a temporary workshop.

There are many ways of solving the workspace problem. To avoid having to cut up large sheets or long boards for example, bring an accurate cutting list to your timber merchant and ask him to cut the pieces to size. They are then easier to handle and transport and require less room to work with at home.

Initially, tool and timber storage may not be a problem. A small box stored under the bed or in a cupboard will hold a few basic tools but with the accumulation of more tools and a small supply of timber and hardware, you will have to consider ways of storing them in a convenient and safe place, away from the reach of all children. The best solution may be to build a worktable which can be used for woodworking as well as sewing and various other hobbies. A family workroom can become a pleasant place where everyone can take a turn to work.

Alternatively you can easily make a temporary work area with a fold-down work bench or with a pair of fold-up trestles which hang away on the wall.

Most of the projects in this book are quite small and can be made on the kitchen table if necessary. In short, do not let the lack of space stop you from making things; if you enjoy woodworking you will manage to find the room.

It is important to form the right work habits from the very beginning. Whether you work in the kitchen or in a large workshop you should always try to hang up the tools as you go along. It is maddening to spend minutes walking around the room looking for the hammer that you just put down. Hang it up or put it away in its box, and you will know exactly where it is when you need it.

The same rule applies to cleaning up. If you work in the spare room you obviously can not leave sawdust all over the floor, but will have to clean up as you work. It is the same in a workshop. Sawdust, shavings and woodscraps left on the floor are a fire hazard and also dangerous as the scraps are easy to trip over. Keep a cardboard box handy for the larger

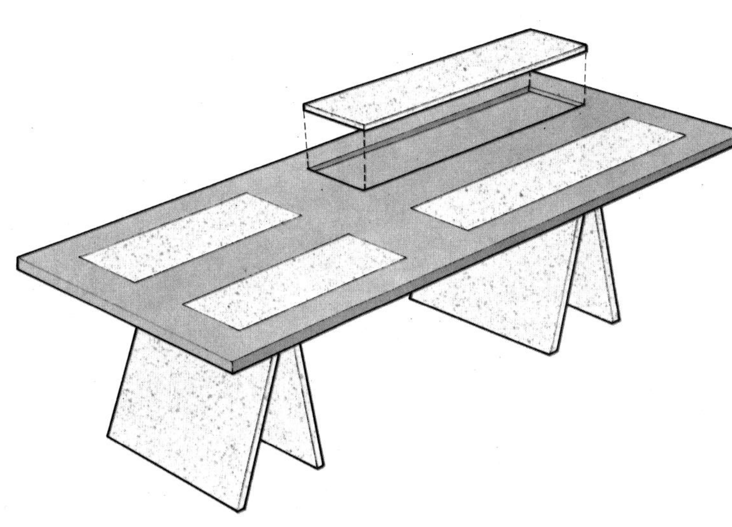

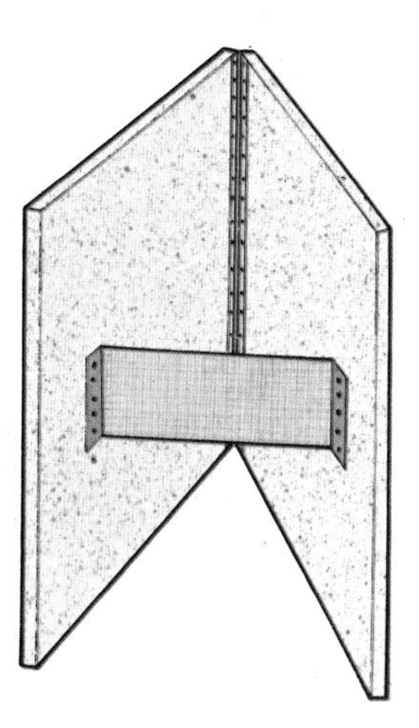

RIGHT: A panel door makes a perfectly good surface for woodworking, but if you use one you should fill in the recesses with hardboard or chipboard to ensure that the surface is flush. Supporting the table is a pair of sturdy fold-away trestles, useful additions in any workshop. This trestle is made of chipboard pieces joined along the top inside edge with a continuous hinge screwed into the edge of the chipboard. Upholstery webbing glued to the centre gives the trestle support.

off-cuts. When the box is full discard all but the really useful pieces. Most workshops have an endless problem with offcuts. Saving too many means lost time looking through a large pile for the right one; throwing them away means having to cut off a new piece when you may only need a small bit. You will develop your own rules as you go along according to the amount of space you have and the amount of work you will be doing.

The temporary work area

The simplest temporary work surface is a sturdy kitchen table on which you can mount a clamp-on type vice for making small projects such as the trivet dishrack or shelf unit detailed in this book (see pages 64 and 77).

Another useful idea is to use a solid door to make a temporary work surface. Nail pieces of hardboard in the panels to make the surface smooth and screw a 6mm sheet of hardboard on top to make a smooth, even work surface. Alternatively you can buy flush-faced solid doors from a timber merchant. Sometimes they have slightly damaged doors, which are sold more cheaply.

There are two convenient ways to support the door to make a temporary store-away surface. First you can make two simple trestles out of 12mm chipboard, continuous hinges and short lengths of fabric upholstery webbing. Cut out holes near the top for convenient handles and also for hanging the trestles out of the way on a wall when they are not needed. The door and trestle can easily double as an extra desk or a dining table, by painting it a bright, attractive colour.

For storing in a narrow hallway, you can attach the door to a batten on the wall with sturdy hinges and drop it down when not in use. For support along the front edges, attach 50 × 50mm softwood legs with a special bracket which allows you to fold the legs up under the door.

To hold the work on temporary work surfaces use G-cramps to hold down flat pieces such as pieces of plywood. Cut small pieces of wood with a bench hook. For instructions on making a bench hook see page 23. You can also buy small cramp-on vices which are easy to take off when putting the worktop away.

Most tools and hardware can be stored away in a small tool box made from offcuts of 19mm plywood, or you can make a simple nailed-together tool box (to hang on the wall) out of 12mm plywood with 6mm plywood back and doors. Put in shelves for storing planes, drill bits and hardware. Add racks for hanging chisels, and screwdrivers. A convenient way to hang most tools is to drill a 9mm diameter hole at a slight angle and glue in a short length of dowel to hang the tool.

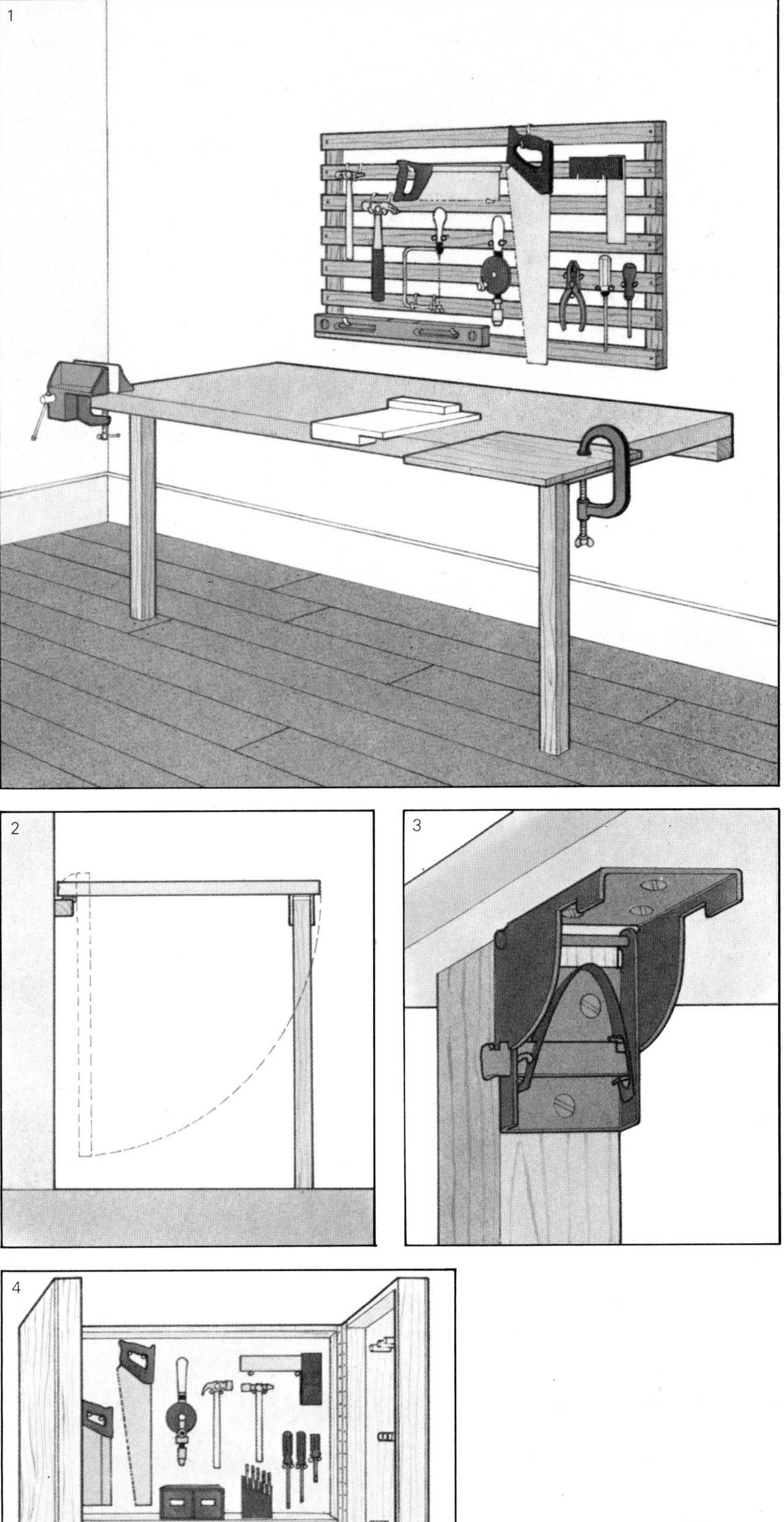

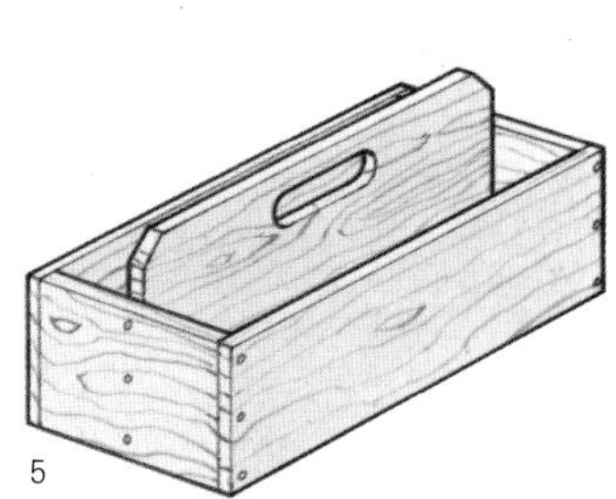

The workshop

The ideal workshop has yet to be designed but for those who are lucky enough to have the space in a shed, garage or basement to create a permanent workshop, there are many simple ideas to make it as efficient and convenient as possible.

Every workshop should have a good sturdy workbench. You can buy a beech woodworking bench but these are now extremely expensive. As an inexpensive alternative follow the instructions on page 48 to make a simple but sturdy screw-together workbench.

The workshop should also have ample storage for lengths of wood and pieces of plywood. Site brackets on the wall for storing wood horizontally. Store large sheets vertically against the wall, standing them on battens to keep them clean and dry. A large cardboard box for offcuts is also convenient, and a good rubbish bin is essential.

Some tools, like planes, should be stored away in a cabinet whenever possible to keep them free from dust, but some tools like clamps, screwdrivers and saws are best stored on pegs on the wall or on pegboard within easy reach.

If possible provide a surface along a wall with cabinets underneath for keeping larger tools such as power saws out of the way. Old kitchen cabinets are perfect for this. Paint them and add a solid top for a very useful workshop cabinet.

It is also convenient to have a couple of trestles or a Workmate hung on the wall to be used when cutting long pieces of timber or large sheets of plywood.

Everyone will work out his own workshop according to the available space, time and money but provide plenty of storage and shelf space for the hundreds of small objects that accumulate around the shop.

Whatever the size of the shop, keep it clean. A dirty, messy shop is difficult and dangerous to work in and it is also a fire hazard. If possible forbid smoking in the workshop, and keep a bucket of water or an extinguisher handy in case a small fire should start. Remember that burning plastics give off poisonous fumes.

It is also important to make sure that there is adequate lighting and ventilation. If dust accumulates it can form an explosive mixture which can flash over a considerable distance. When working with finishing materials and some glues such as contact adhesives, keep a window or door open to let out the fumes. Chemicals, paints and glues should always be stored away out of reach of children when not in use to prevent accidents.

These safety measures are only common sense, always a requirement in woodworking. They also make the job easier.

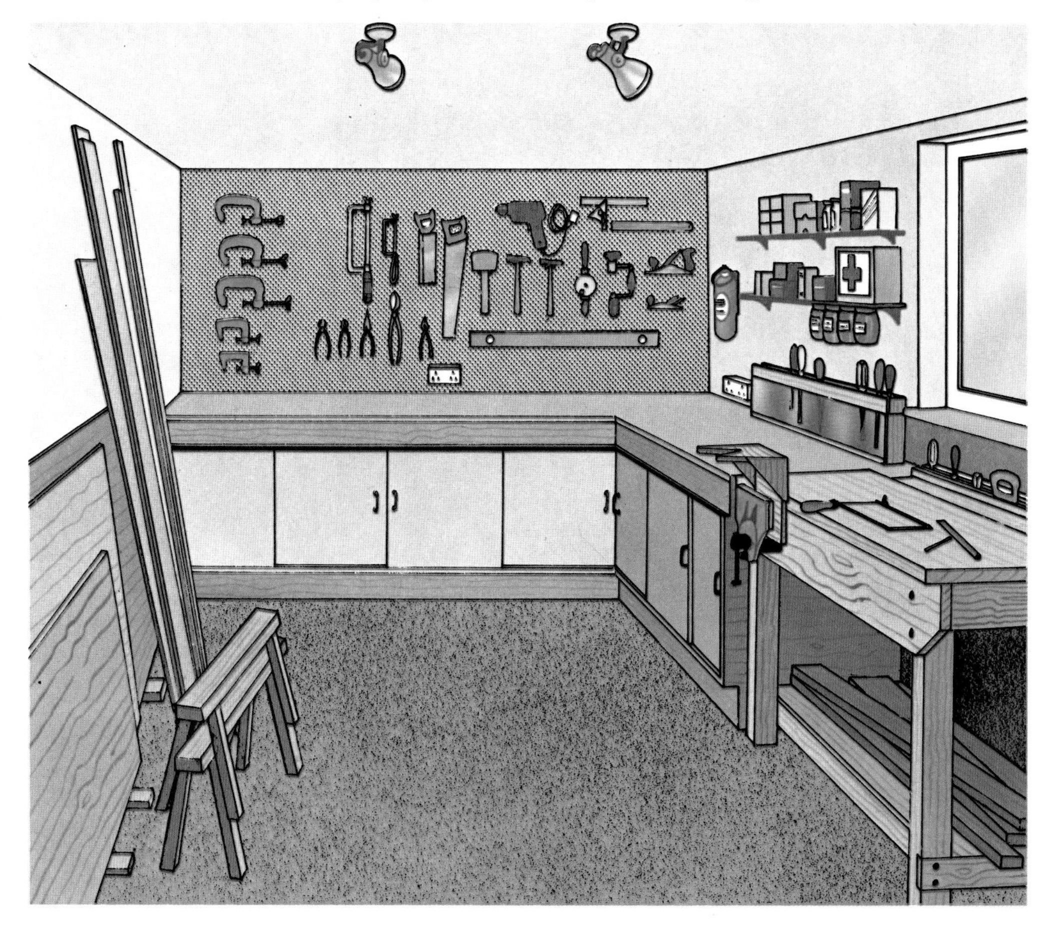

A well-fitted workshop requires ample storage space, sturdy benches, good lighting and plenty of space to cut up large sheets of plywood. It is always convenient to hang the tools on peg-boards within easy reach. To establish the general layout, trace an outline of the tools which will be placed on the pegboard immediately behind where each will go. Screws and nails are best stored in jars with the lid screwed to the underside of a shelf.

Storing timber and large sheet materials can be a problem. The best way is to store the sheets vertically on their sides, placing them on battens laid on the floor to keep them dry. If possible store all timber away from the work bench to minimize the danger of having it fall on you or your work.

Project: Making a rack

Cut the four pieces of wood and glue them together, using the short pieces as spacers. Put a G-cramp at each spacer and leave the glue to set. Drill a hole at either end and hang up the rack with the brass screws. The one illustrated was designed to store kitchen utensils, but you could make something similar for your tools.

There are several other handy ways to store tools and wood at home. A pegboard is always useful for hanging up tools. Make a more attractive version by screwing 19 × 38mm slots to two uprights with a space between each to fit hooks made by bending wire coat hangers.

You can also make a large drawer on castors to fit under the bed for storing tools, hardware and small pieces of wood.

Storing wood in a limited space is always a problem. It can stand up in the back of a cupboard or lie under a bed, but a better solution may be to attach a few brackets high up on the wall in the hallway to store the wood horizontally out of sight.

A most ingenious device for a temporary workbench is a metal fold-up bench called a Workmate. It is a small, sturdy worktop and holds almost all sizes of wood firmly in its jaws. It folds up in a few seconds and hangs out of the way on the wall. Even if you have a proper workbench a Workmate is often useful as a temporary surface and as a place to hold an awkward shape such as a door.

Tool rack

Things to buy:

One piece of 9 × 25mm planed softwood approximately 1m long, cut into two pieces 450mm long and two pieces 35mm long
Woodworking glue
Two No. 8 brass screws with matching cup washers to hang the rack to the wall. Use long screws with fibre wall plugs when attaching it directly to a masonry wall

Tools required:

Tenon saw
G-cramps
Drill
Screwdriver

ABOVE: *This simple construction holding kitchen utensils would serve equally well as a rack for tools in the workshop. It is made from lengths of softwood glued together with spacer pieces and then screwed to the wall with brass screws.*

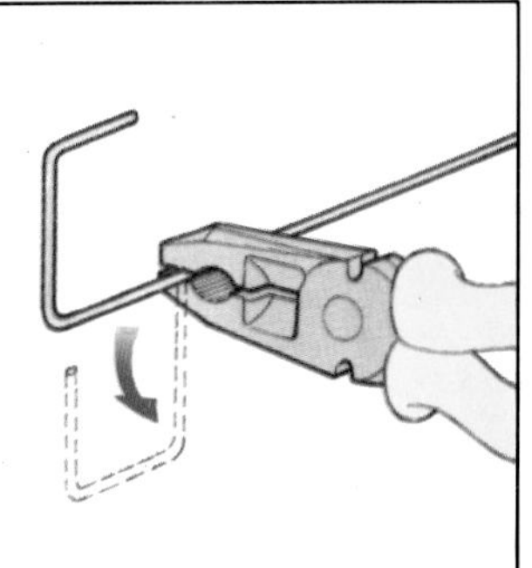

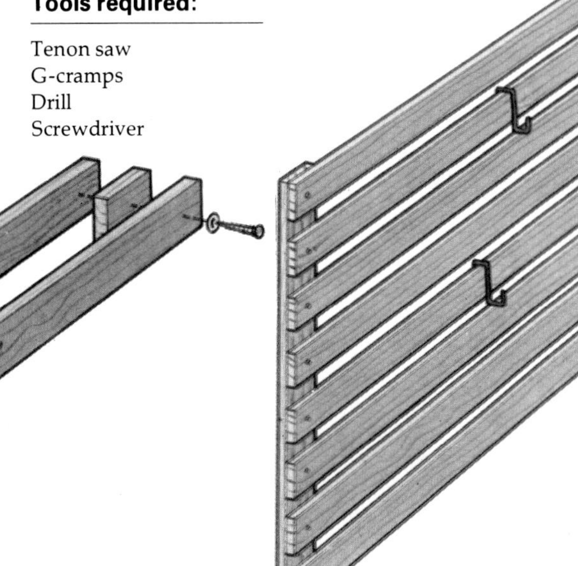

FAR LEFT: *The spacer is made by sandwiching small blocks of wood between battens of the same width and depth and then screwing the three layers together, as shown.*

CENTRE: *The slatted tool rack shown on page 45 is not only simple to make but extremely versatile, since you can place the hooks where you want them.*

ABOVE: *To make the hooks, bend straight lengths of wire coathangers to fit over the slats.*

Project: Making a workbench

This workbench is ample size for almost all types of work. The sturdy top is made up from three layers of plywood. The bottom two 19mm thick layers are screwed down to the rails and also hold the vice and bench stop. The replaceable top 6.5mm layer is simply pinned on top so that it hides the screws and the coach bolt fixings for the vice. It can be replaced in minutes when the surface gets old and dirty.

There is a well along the back to keep tools and shavings out of the way when working on a large project.

The bench is fitted with a sturdy woodworker's vice bolted to the top and a retractable bench stop for use as a stop when planing lengths of wood.

The tool rack along the back is convenient for storing saws, chisels and other tools within easy reach.

The difficult part about making the bench is cutting the pieces to length. If possible, take the cutting list to a timber merchant and have him cut the timber, but be sure to take along a tape measure to check his work. Do not accept pieces if they are not correctly cut.

Cutting list

Material	Description	Size or length
A 19mm plywood	top	450 × 1450mm
B 19mm plywood	top	600 × 1450mm
C 19mm plywood	shelf	415 × 1220mm
D 19mm plywood	back	440 × 1220mm
E 6.5mm plywood	top	450 × 1450mm
F 75 × 75mm softwood	legs	800mm long, 4 pieces
G 32 × 100mm softwood	long rails	1180mm long, 3 pieces
H 32 × 100mm softwood	end rails	550mm long, 4 pieces
I 38 × 150mm softwood	front rail	1360mm long, 1 piece
J 12 × 50mm softwood	tool rack	1450mm long, 2 pieces
K 12 × 50mm softwood	tool rack spacers	75mm long, 3 pieces

Hardware

40 No. 10 steel c'sunk screws, 63mm long
3 No. 12 steel c'sunk screws, 25mm long
16 No. 10 chrome cup washers
15 No. 8 brass c'sunk screws, 38mm long
15 No. 8 brass cup washers
10 panel pins, 32mm long
20 panel pins, 19mm long

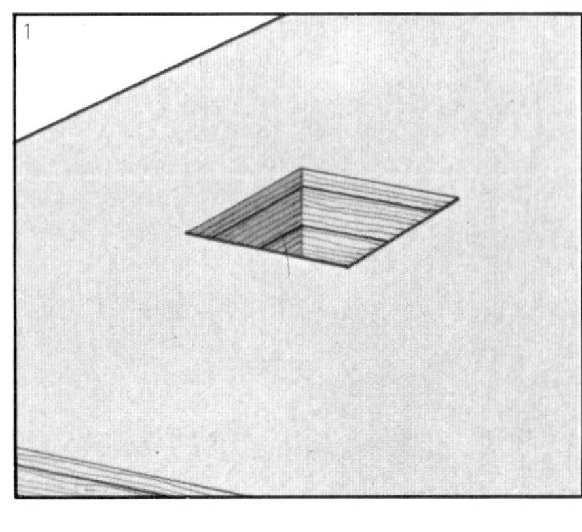

The workbench. **1** *A retractable bench stop fits into a square hole in the bench surface.* **2** *With the vice as a guide, cut out a recess in the front of the bench rail to hold the vice in position.* **3** *You can store small tools in the well and larger ones in the tool rack.* **4** *The side and back rails of the bench screw into the leg for more support.* **5** *The leg and side of the bottom shelf are joined together by a halving joint.*

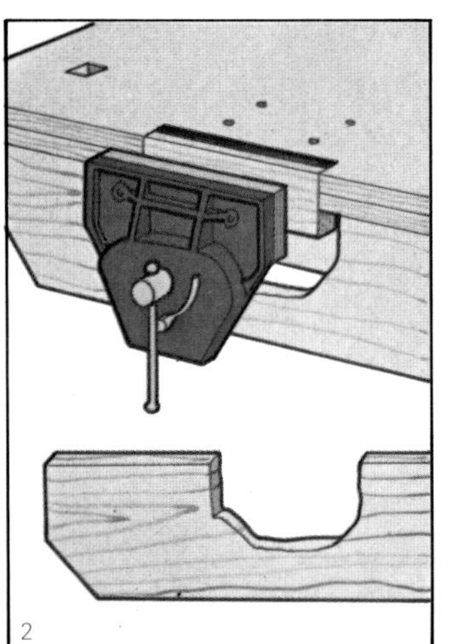

Procedure

1. Cut all pieces to size. Mark them with letters A, B, C etc.
2. Cut two halving joints in each leg F. Rails do not require cutting.
3. Assemble two end frames. Place end rails H in slots cut in legs and attach with two 63mm No. 10 screws with chrome cup washers in each joint.
4. Assemble basic frame by screwing the long rails G to end frames with 63mm No. 10 screws without cup washers. Check connections with try-square.
5. Screw down plywood shelf C to rails H with three 38mm No. 8 brass screws with cup washers, at either end.
6. Screw plywood back D to legs F with three 38mm No. 8 brass screws and cup washers at either end.
7. Glue and pin tops A and B together using the 32mm panel pins. Keep front edges together to create the well at the back.
8. Fit vice and bench stop to top. Cut out notch for vice and use coach bolts and plywood packing underneath to fit vice. Cut rectangular opening before fitting bench stop with three 25mm No. 12 screws.
9. With vice and bench stop fitted, screw top down to end rails H with 63mm No. 10 screws and to back rail G with three 38mm brass screws with cup washers.
10. Cut corners off ends of front rail I, then cut out notch for vice by cutting out approximate shape and then doing final cutting of details by trial and error. Screw front rails to legs with two 63mm No. 10 screws at each end. Hide screw fixings either by counter boring and plugging or by filling countersunk hole.
11. Cut out hole in 6.5mm top E for bench stop, then pin down the top with 19mm panel pins. Sink pins well below the surface with nail punch.
12. Attach tool rack to back of plywood top B. Screw one 63mm No. 10 screw through two strips J separated by spacer K at either end and at middle.
13. Sand and finish workbench.

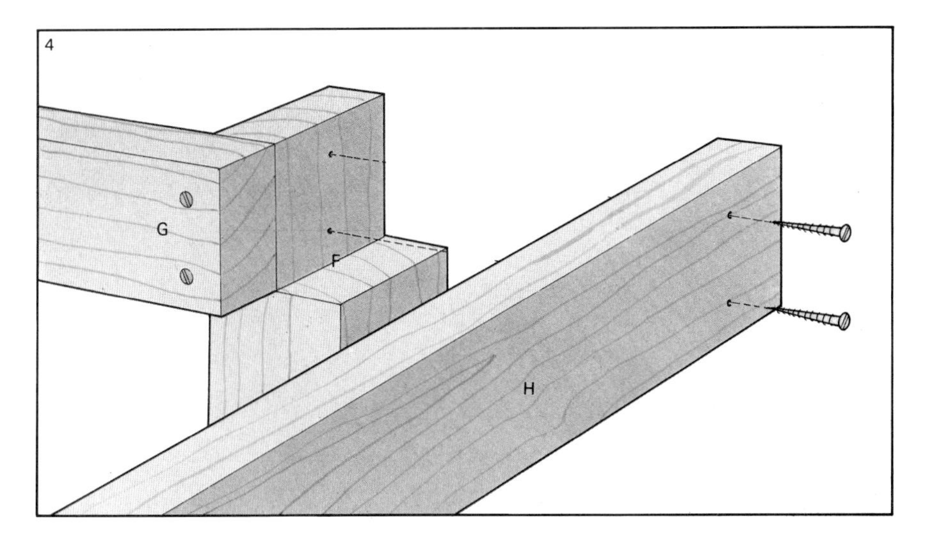

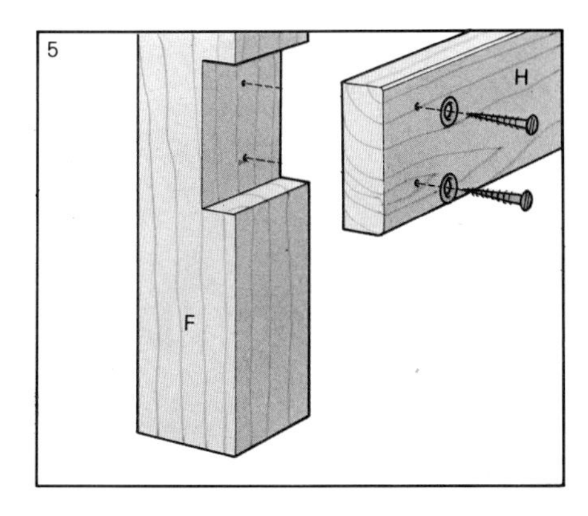

RIGHT: *Not only is the workbench you can make very good looking but it is both sturdy and extremely functional. A bench such as this enables you to work on a firm, flat surface with all your tools at hand. Note the wood which has been stored on the lower level and the tools slotted into the rack behind.*

Adhesives, nails and screws

There are so many different ways of joining wood together that even the most experienced woodworkers can not master them all. Most projects do not require complicated joints such as dovetails and mortise and tenons.

Before making joints requiring adhesives, nails or screws, check with the tables in this chapter to find the right type for the job.

Adhesives: choosing the right one for the job

Adhesives are widely used not only to glue wood to wood joints but also to join materials such as rubber, metal, glass, fabric and even stone. The chart below shows a wide variety of glues, but for general woodworking, only two or three types are normally required. In choosing an adhesive keep in mind several factors:

1. Choose the glue that is suitable for the materials to be joined. PVA woodworking glue is best for ordinary wood to wood joints but a strong epoxy adhesive may be required to bond glass to glass or wood to metal.

2. Consider the strength of the joint: the corner mitre joint of a picture frame does not have to be particularly strong, so general-purpose PVA adhesive is quite adequate. The dowelled framework of chairs, on the other hand, has to stand up to a lot of strain, and a stronger synthetic resin adhesive is more suitable.

3. Always keep in mind the site of the glued joints. The most important consideration is moisture. For projects that will undergo exposure to rain or water, such as garden furniture or kitchen and bathroom articles, use a waterproof adhesive such as a synthetic resin.

The basic tool kit should include a medium-sized container of general purpose PVA woodworking glue, small amounts of epoxy cement for special jobs, and synthetic resin for waterproof joints. A tube of quick-drying cellulose glue for model-making and small repairs is also useful but it is best to buy other adhesives, such as contact cement, for specific jobs. The new, instant glues which bond in seconds should not be used for woodwork; they can be dangerous to use and are not necessary.

Gluing techniques

Read the manufacturer's instructions before using any glue. The surfaces to be glued must be clean, dry and free from grease. Most glues should be applied at room temperature and normal moisture conditions, otherwise they may take longer to set and might not set at all.

Apply the adhesives evenly, usually to only one contact surface, with a brush or a spreader, then clamp the pieces together moderately tightly. Too much glue or too much clamping pressure will result in most of the glue squeezing out on to the wood and the bench below.

Develop good habits when you glue, particularly for large jobs. Mix up only as much glue as is required. Once the glue is applied, carefully clean off the excess glue before it sets. Finally, clean all brushes and applicators immediately so that they are ready for the next time you need them.

Adhesives

Type	Description	Typical applications	Strength	Water resistance	Which materials
Animal or Scotch glues	Old-fashioned woodworking adhesive made from hides and bones. Glue is melted in a special glue pot and is then applied hot. It hardens quickly at room temperature.	Formerly used for most woodworking joints. Particularly useful for gluing down veneers because glue can be softened with application of heat, such as an iron, for adjustment or repair of veneer.	Good	Poor	Wood to wood
PVA (polyvinyl acetate)	White liquid glue available in plastic containers for easy spreading. Clamp work for 20-30 minutes while glue sets. Dries completely hard in 24 hours. Dries clear, but wipe off excess glue with a damp cloth before glue sets.	Most versatile woodworking adhesive, used for all interior woodworking joints and repairs.	Good	Fair	Wood, cork, leather, fabric, and paper to wood.
Synthetic resin	Generally available as powder containing both glue and hardener. Mix with water according to instructions. Work must be clamped for 4-6 hours depending on room temperature. Wipe off excess glue with cloth moistened with warm water after clamping.	Excellent gap-filling properties makes resin glue ideal for loose-fitting joints in furniture making. Also used for boat-building and other outdoor projects.	Excellent	Very Good	Wood to wood
Epoxy	Available in pairs of small tubes. Resin and hardener are mixed together before use. Quick-drying type sets in 10 minutes, others in about 6 hours. Avoid contact with skin. Clean with methylated spirit.	Expense limits application to small jobs such as joining metal, glass, ceramics or stone.	Excellent	Excellent	Glues almost everything. Wood, metal, glass or plastic to wood. Metal, glass, plastic, or stone to metal. Glass to glass.
Contact cement	Rubber-based adhesive applied to both surfaces and allowed to touch-dry before joining with firm hand pressure. Instant joint means no cramping is required. Surfaces cannot be moved once joined. (New types allow minor adjustment.) Clean with special solvents sold by glue makers or with acetone or nail varnish removers.	Generally used for fixing plastic laminates to counter tops. Also used for small repairs including wood joints not subject to much stress.	Good	Good	Glues almost any hard materials, particularly plastics and plastic laminates to wood.
Cellulose	Plastic-based adhesive available in small tubes. Dries very quickly, is therefore used for fixing small awkwardly shaped pieces. Dries clear. Remove excess glue immediately with acetone or nail varnish remover.	Used extensively for model building and small household repairs, such as fixing broken china.	Good	Good	Glass, china, plastics to glass. China, plastics to wood.

Nails and screws

Nails

Nails are available in a variety of sizes, shapes and materials. Unlike screws, which actually grip the wood, nails hold by friction. A nail driven into wood forces the fibres apart, and because of the very tight fit, the friction between the nail and the wood holds the nail in place. If the wood splits, which often happens particularly near the end of a board, there is little friction and therefore little holding power. Oval nails are less likely to split the wood.

Most nails can be bought either by weight or in small individual packages, but it is more economical to buy them loose and store them in labelled boxes or jars. The most useful types and sizes are round or oval wire nails in lengths from about 38 to 63mm and panel pins in lengths from about 19 to 32mm. Buying other types and sizes as necessary will soon give you a good selection.

For most applications, steel nails are suitable, but for projects where these are likely to rust and discolour the wood, use galvanised nails or aluminium nails, although these are not available in as wide a range of sizes.

If in doubt about which type or size of nail to buy, seek the advice of a hardware merchant. Page 71 gives further information and details about nailed joints.

Screws

Length and gauge Screws are available in a number of sizes, gauges, materials and head types. The size is specified by the length and the gauge, which is a measure of the shank diameter and is referred to by the number (No.). The larger the number, the heavier the screw. The most useful sizes range from about 19mm to about 63mm, but there are also many uses for screws as small as 6.5mm in diameter and as long as 152mm. It is often much more economical to buy screws in complete boxes of 200 or in half boxes of 100. They are also sold loose or in packages of ten, when only a small number is needed.

It is important to use the correct length of screw to fix two pieces of wood. It must project far enough into the second piece to have sufficient strength but not extend through the other side.

Page 53 lists the use of screws and ways to determine the required lengths.

Materials used for screws Steel screws are the most common but brass screws, although they are not as strong, are more attractive and do not rust.

Screws are also available with special finishes such as chrome and black japanned, although

Nails for general woodworking

Type	Description and use	Generally available lengths (mm)
Round wire nail	General purpose steel nail. Usually for rough construction jobs. Larger sizes likely to split the wood. Some sizes available galvanised.	20-150
Oval wire nail	Used in construction and joinery. Oval shape is less likely to split wood.	20-150
Lost head nail (round or oval)	For joinery and laying floor boards. Less obtrusive head is either left flush or punched below surface.	40-75 round 20-150 oval
Floorboard nail	Sturdy rectangular section nail used to fix down floorboards. Does not split the wood.	38-75
Panel pin	Thin nail with very narrow head used in general joinery and cabinet making for jobs requiring small hidden fixing, such as attaching mouldings, cabinet backs.	12-38

Other useful nails:

Type	Description and use	Generally available lengths (mm)
Hardboard nail	Copper-finished nail with extra strength to go through hardboard. Diamond-shaped head is driven into board.	18-100
Masonry nail	Extra hard nails used for fixing in masonry and concrete. Available in small packages.	6-30
Tack	Old or "improved" styles. Used to fix fabric, webbing or carpet to wood.	3-12
Chair nails	Available in brass, bronze, chrome or antique finish. Used as decorative nail in upholstery.	20-75
Annular nail	Steel nail with fine ridges. Used in joinery where extra holding strength is required.	25-75
Staple	Used for fixing wire to wood. Particularly for fencing and upholstery. Also available galvanised.	12-38

not in all sizes or head shapes. It is best to check availability with a large hardware shop before planning to use a special screw.

Head types Countersunk head screws are screwed in so that the head is flush with (countersunk) or slightly below (counterbored) the surface.

Round head screws are used for fixing sheet metal to wood or as a decorative fixing. They are available in steel and also in a black japanned finish or in more expensive brass or chrome finishes. The raised countersunk head is a decorative head used mostly to fix hardware to furniture.

Slotted and cross-slotted screw heads Most screws have a single slot for use with ordinary screwdrivers, but where the screw is difficult to site, the head is often damaged, particularly on the softer brass screws.

Cross-slotted or Phillips head screw heads, for use with special cross-slotted screwdrivers which come in three sizes, are much less likely to be damaged as the screwdriver has a much firmer grip on the screw.

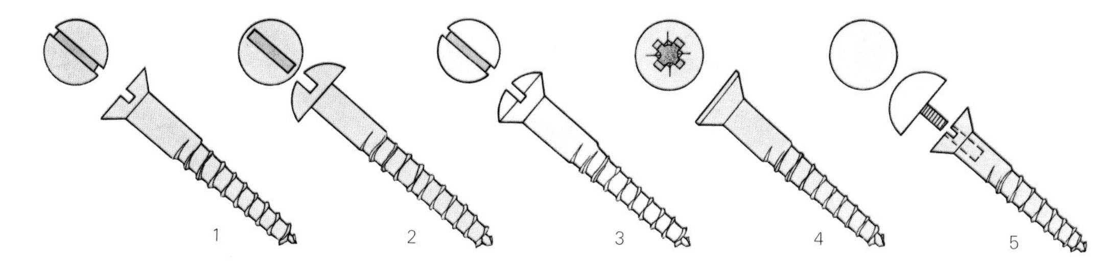

Screws: Readily available sizes

Countersunk steel

mm	in	Shank numbers 3	4	6	8	10	12	14	16
9	3/8	o	o	o					
12	1/2	o	o	o	o				
15	5/8	o	o	o	o				
19	3/4	o	o	o	o	o	o		
25	1	o	o	o	o	o	o	o	
32	1 1/4		o	o	o	o	o	o	
38	1 1/2		o	o	o	o	o	o	o
44	1 3/4			o	o	o	o	o	o
50	2			o	o	o	o	o	o
57	2 1/4			o	o	o	o	o	
63	2 1/2			o	o	o	o	o	o
76	3			o	o	o	o	o	o
89	3 1/2				o	o	o	o	o
101	4				o	o	o	o	o

Countersunk brass

mm	in	Shank numbers 3	4	6	8	10	12	14
9	3/8	o	o	o				
12	1/2	o	o	o	o			
15	5/8	o	o	o	o			
19	3/4		o	o	o			
25	1		o	o	o	o	o	
32	1 1/4			o	o	o	o	
38	1 1/2			o	o	o	o	o
44	1 3/4				o	o	o	
50	2			o	o	o	o	o
63	2 1/2				o	o	o	o
76	3				o	o	o	o

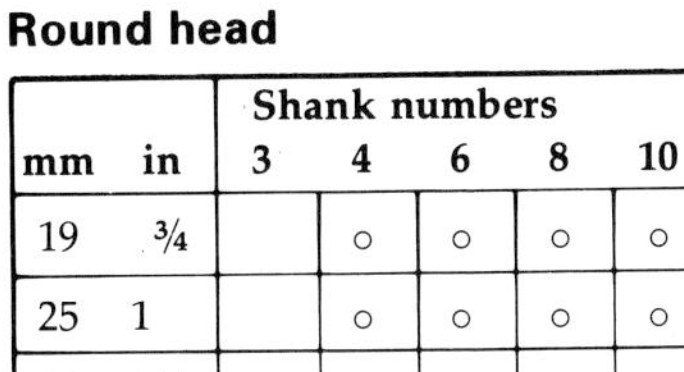

Round head

mm	in	Shank numbers 3	4	6	8	10	12	14
19	3/4		o	o	o	o		
25	1		o	o	o	o	o	
32	1 1/4			o	o	o	o	
38	1 1/2			o	o	o	o	
50	2			o	o	o	o	o
63	2 1/2				o	o	o	o
76	3					o	o	

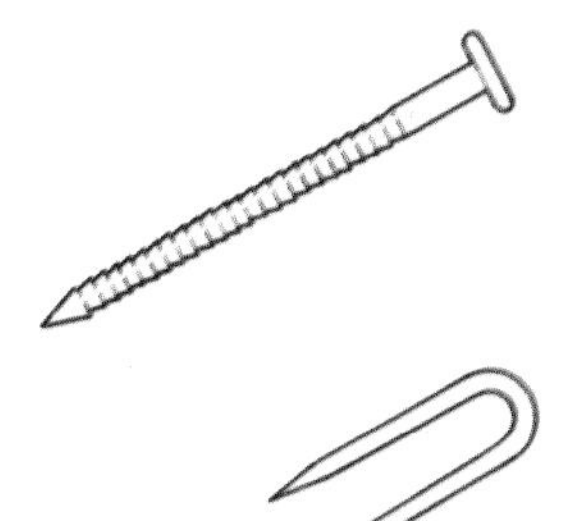

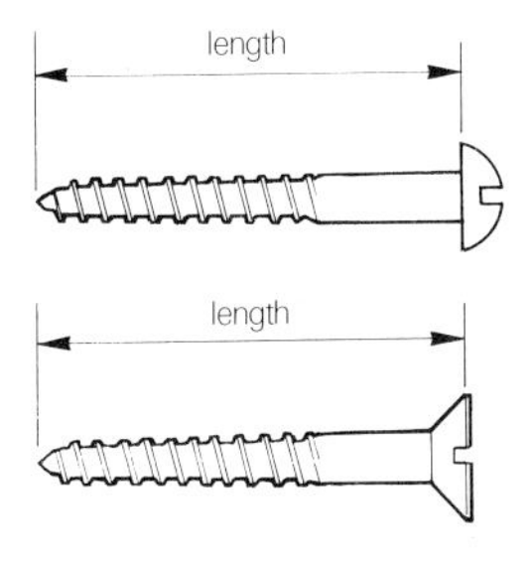

ABOVE, FROM LEFT: *The various screw types available: countersunk, round head, raised countersunk. Phillips head and dome-covered. When measuring a round head screw* **(top)**, *do not include the head as part of its length.*

Preparing timber

In any project, from the simplest shelf to the most complicated piece of furniture, certain basic measuring and marking techniques are always used. In marking out the length of a simple board, for example, it is essential to check that the starting end is square.

The importance of these techniques and the accuracy required varies from project to project. A simple wall shelf could be slightly overlong and not exactly square, but if that shelf has to fit exactly inside a cabinet the ends must be straight and accurate. It is important to learn the correct methods so that they come naturally.

Most softwoods can be bought already planed up, with square sides.

It is much easier to use only planed wood and save the time and effort of planing the four sides by hand. Hardwoods are usually only sold in the sawn state so if you plan to use, say, a piece of mahogany, it is best to find a local workshop to plane it accurately on a machine.

Checking for straightness Even though the wood has already been planed it may, after lying in the garage or house for a while, tend to bow slightly, so first check by sighting along the length that the boards are straight. If any have warped or bowed badly they will have to be discarded, although a slightly bowed board may be used or it can be corrected by planing along the bowed edge with a long plane. Warped boards can be cut up for use as wedges and packing pieces.

Marking the face and edge Choose the best face and the best side of each board and mark them with a pencilled loop on the face carried over to the best side. These marks are important because all subsequent measurements and markings will be made from these two sides.

This may sound tedious but without a system of marking, in making a table support with four legs and four rails, for example, there would be no way of keeping track of which sides face inwards and which face outwards.

Marking and cutting to length For larger jobs it is best to prepare a cutting list indicating the number of pieces and the length of each piece you will need.

Always cut the longest piece first and the shortest last, so if you make a mistake and cut the first piece a bit short there is usually enough wood to cut another; the slightly short piece can be used for the next shorter size.

Before cutting the boards to length check one end of the board with a try-square. Unless it is already square, mark a square line at least 50mm in from the end, then saw the board off along the line, with a tenon saw. With one end square you can now measure off each piece, mark it with a try-square and cut it to length.

The saw cut will remove about 2mm of wood, so you must saw on the *other* side of the line to make the piece exactly the length you have measured. (See page 22).

Planing the ends For some work the ends can be left rough sawn, but for furniture the ends should be planed smooth. Cut the boards one or two millimetres overlength to allow for planing off the ends.

Hold the board vertically in a vice and use a block plane to plane the end smooth. Remember to plane in toward the centre from either end to avoid the wood breaking or chipping along the edges.

Plywood, blockboard and chipboard

Plywood and other sheet materials can be prepared in the same way, starting from two edges which have been checked for squareness.

Mark the other two sides to length, using a large try-square or marking the length at both ends and drawing the line with a straight-edge.

Cut the pieces just a millimetre or so too large and plane the sides straight to the exact size. To cut larger pieces use a power circular saw where possible. See page 39 for a guide to precise cuts.

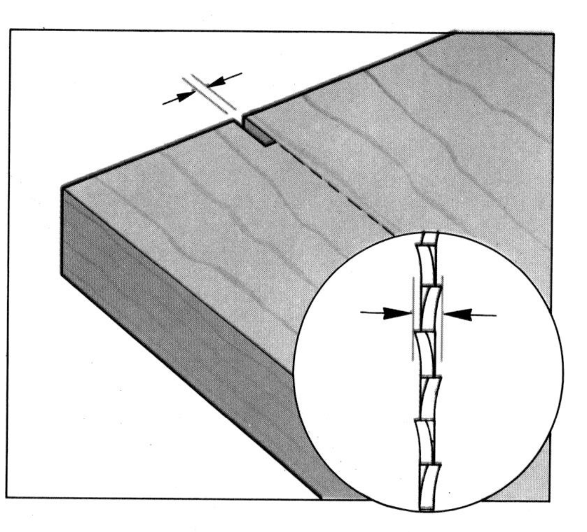

RIGHT: *The kerf is the tiny width of wood removed by the saw blade. Note the jagged effect this has when seen in close up. It is important to saw on the 'waste' side of the marked line so that you finish with the right size.*

OPPOSITE: *Before starting any woodworking job, make sure you have all the materials you will need and measure them carefully. It will save time and problems if you adopt this very good habit; it will also make the job more enjoyable.*

2 lengths 50mm x 50mm.
2 lengths 50mm x 25mm.
Box of nails
Box of screws

Basic joints

The most important thing in woodworking is to choose the right joint for the job: it is a waste of effort to put together a garden fence with the mortise and tenon joints used in fine furniture. Each joint has its specific application, so whether you use a dowel joint or simply nail the pieces of wood together depends entirely on where the joint is and how strong it should be.

Wood can be joined either by old-fashioned interlocking glued wood joints such as the halving, dowel or mitre joint, or by nails, screws and other special fittings. These methods are all described in this chapter. Mortise and tenon and dovetail joints are more complicated to make and are not covered here.

Whatever method of joining is used, it is essential to have the wood planed so that it is straight and square.

Halving joints

The halving joint is quite simple to make and has many applications. It is made by cutting away half the thickness from each piece so that the two pieces fit flush when they are joined. The two pieces are usually clamped and glued together. Depending on the use, the joint can be reinforced slightly with a few panel pins or perhaps screws.

Halving joints cannot be made in timber less than 20mm thick, as cutting away half the thickness would then leave less than 10mm of wood, which would break quite easily.

Marking a halving joint Mark the two sections to be cut away. Lay one piece on the other and check that they are perfectly square with a try-square. Using a sharp pencil, mark the outline on both the top and the bottom piece. Take the top piece away and score across the pencil line with either a marking-knife or another sharp knife, using a try-square as a guide.

Mark the depth of the cut to be made on each piece; on boards of equal thickness make these marks exactly half the thickness so an equal amount is cut away from both pieces. (On boards of unequal thickness remove sufficient to allow the thinner piece to sit flush.)

Finally, continue the face marks down one side to the half-way line as a guide for the saw.

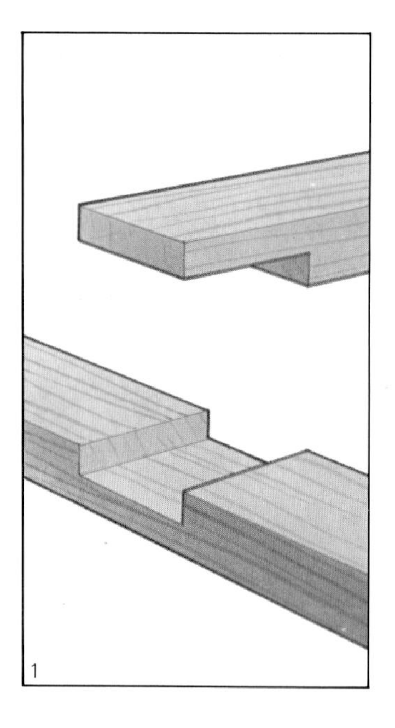

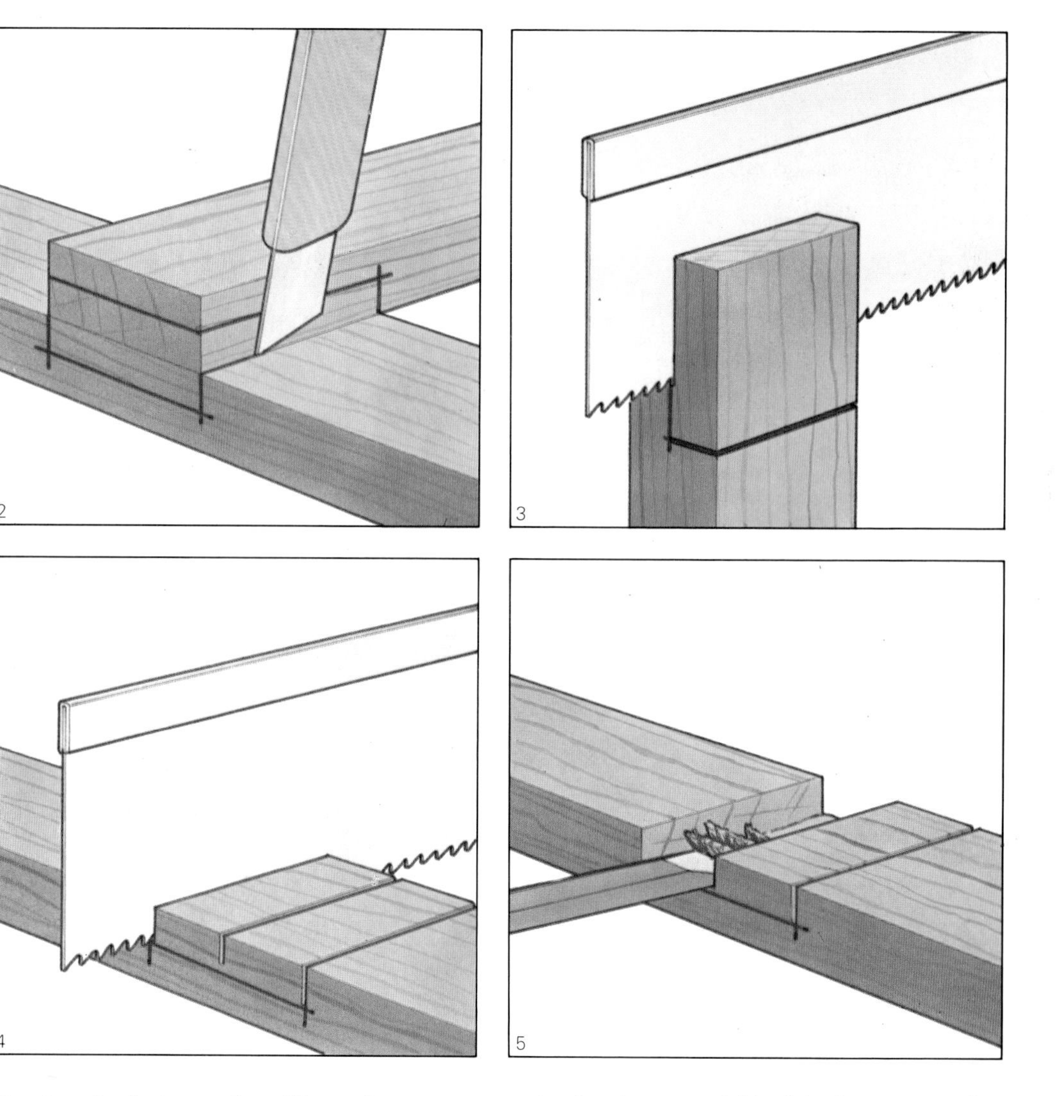

When you are marking and cutting halving joints, take great care to do it accurately so that the pieces fit together tightly **(1)**. *If possible, use a marking knife* **(2)** *instead of a pencil for more accurate cutting lines and when sawing* **(3)**, *remember to cut on the waste side of the line. A joint which is too tight or which does not fit can always be corrected; too loose a joint is difficult to remedy. Make extra saw cuts in the middle of the wood to be removed* **(4)** *as this makes it easier to chisel away the waste wood.*

Cutting the bottom piece Use a sharp tenon saw to make cuts *inside* the lines, i.e. on the waste side, to the half-way line. Make a few extra saw cuts in between to make the wood easier to remove with a chisel.

Use a sharp chisel to cut away the waste, working from both sides to the middle. Cut fine slices, gradually making the cut flat.

Cutting the top piece For a cross-joint the top is cut exactly as the bottom, using a saw and chisel. A T-joint or corner joint can be cut using only the saw. Put the piece in a vice and saw the waste side of the half-way lines, to the exact depth. Be careful not to saw too deeply. Cut off the waste by sawing along the shoulder line made with the marking knife.

No chiselling is required for corner joints; both the top and the bottom pieces can be cut with a tenon saw.

Halving joints can be used to make cross-joints, T-joints and corner joints. These are frequently used in furniture construction and also for making simple doors and frames.

Using halving joints

Corner joints The corner halving joint is a useful substitute for the mitre joint, particularly when a mitre box is not available. It is also stronger than a mitre joint and can be used on light doors. Both parts can be cut using only a saw, which makes it quite easy to make.

If the four corner joints are made accurately the frame should be square. Check the squareness of the frames by measuring diagonals, and adjust if necessary before gluing up. A few panel pins can be used on the joints to keep them rigid.

The simple frame can be used as a door for a kitchen or bathroom cabinet or as a basic picture frame.

For use as a door the frame needs a centre panel made of plywood or other sheet material. You can attach the panel by nailing it directly on to the back of the frame, hiding the edge with a piece of moulding.

Crossed joints The crossed halving joint is stronger than the dowelled cross joint. Both pieces require careful marking and cutting out with a saw and a chisel. Like the other halving joints, it is generally used with the pieces lying flat for frameworks such as doors and screens, but the pieces can just as easily be on edge, and the joints slotted together like the cardboard dividers in a wine crate.

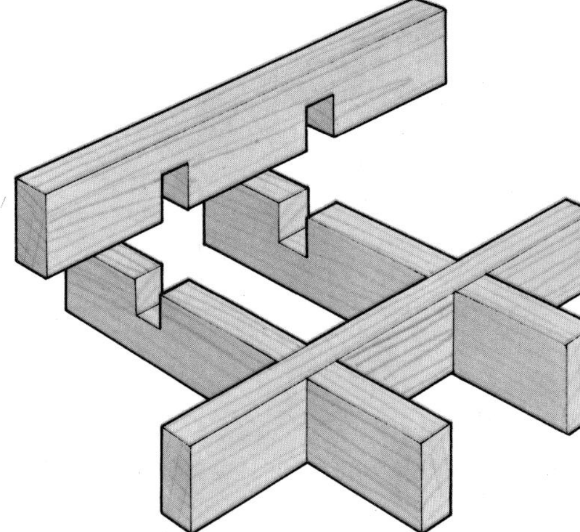

Project: Making a trivet

This is a very simple project. First cut four pieces of 12 × 25 stripping, 150mm long (don't worry if the pieces are not identical).

Mark out the halving joints as above, about 30mm in from each end, being careful to make the joints tight.

Try the pieces for fit, then take them apart and sand before gluing them together. Smooth the ends a little with glasspaper.

This handsome trivet is an excellent first project for mastering the technique of halving joints. The trivet is made from teak, but you could use pine instead; whichever of the two you use, the result provides an attractive item.

Trivet

Things to buy

650mm of 12 × 25mm softwood or hardwood strips
Woodworking glue

Tools needed

Pencil
Saw
6.5 or 9mm wide chisel
Glasspaper

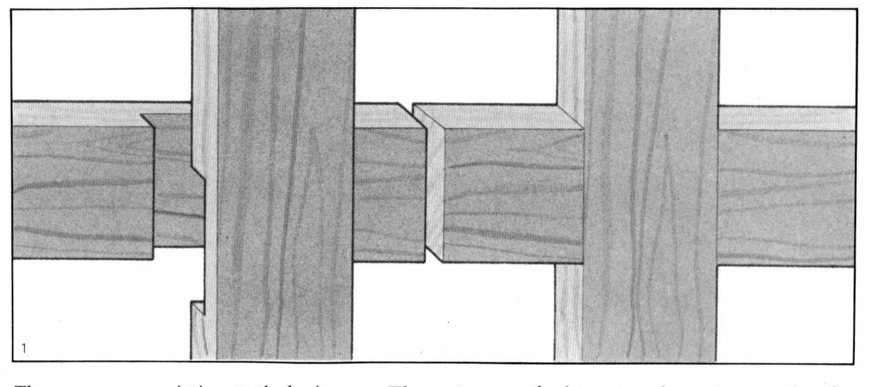

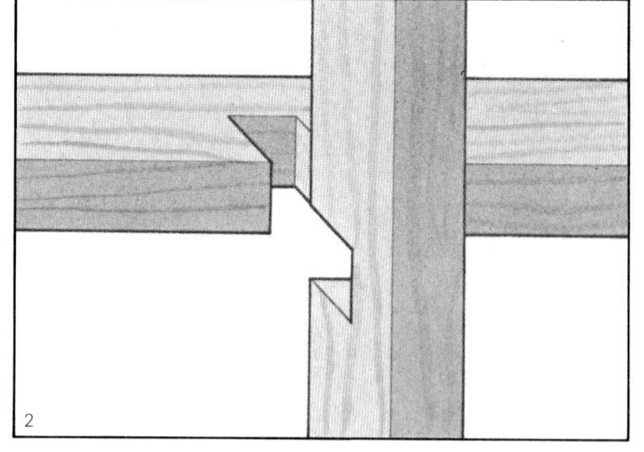

There are many variations to the basic halving joint. **1** *The joint can either be flat with both faces cut away for a flush joint, or for a deeper joint* **(2)** *cut into the timber edges.*

The pieces of this simple spice rack, for example, slot together and are then nailed to the four surrounding pieces. Similarly, larger boards, making up the base of a simple platform bed, can slot together to make up a sturdy and rigid structure.

The ends of the boards can be left exposed with the spaces between used for storage of pillows and blankets, or they can be covered up by screwing on boards of the same depth to form a surround for the base.

T-Joints The T-halving joint is very useful in both furniture making and in general carpentry. Because the joint is neat and flush and quite sturdy it is frequently used, for example, for the rails in old-fashioned tables. It is more often used in light frames such as tall cupboard doors to connect the mid-height cross piece to the sides. These doors are quite easy to make out of ordinary softwood. Use 20mm thick pieces for the frames, keeping the uprights narrower than the cross pieces. The central panels of thin plywood can easily be screwed or nailed to the framework to make it sturdier. The panels can be stained or perhaps covered with a fabric or wallpaper to match the room décor.

You can also make a small ladder, say for a children's bunk bed, using halving T-joints. Use timber at least 25mm thick and reinforce the halving joint with a screw from the back to make it safe to climb on. Look around to see how often the T-joint is used, on large and small items alike. Its sheer simplicity is the key to its usefulness as a joint.

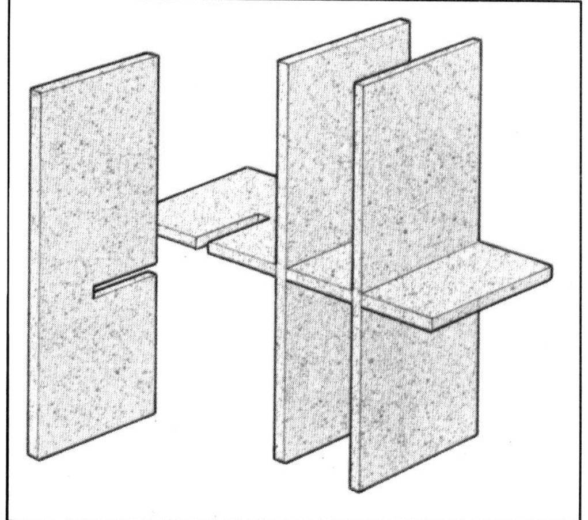

Halving joints are a simple and versatile way of joining timber and sheet materials to make ladders, door frames, shelving units, and other practical household items such as these. The attractive spice shelf **(right)** *is an example of a project that makes use of halving joints which slot together* **(above)** *to form a unit; the shelves are secured by a surround nailed in to the ends of the dividers. To make the shelf even more stable, you can pin a piece of hardboard to the back.*

Curry
Thyme
Sage

Dowel joints

The dowel joint is the modern substitute for the traditional mortise and tenon joint. It is particularly useful for the home handyman, as it requires very few tools and is easy to make accurately. Basically the two pieces of wood are fixed together by short lengths of dowel glued halfway into each piece. The dowels are then hidden when the joint is assembled.

Dowelling is quite straightforward as long as the marking and drilling are done carefully and accurately. The matching holes drilled in the two pieces must line up exactly so that the pieces are flush and straight when the joint is assembled.

Making dowel joints will become quite automatic after a little practice. It is important to do each step slowly and carefully in turn; to develop the right habits for measuring, marking, drilling and assembling the joints.

Dowel pegs Ready-made dowel pegs are obtainable in three diameters, 6.5mm, 9mm and 12mm; and in various lengths from 19mm to about 75mm. The ends are bevelled or chamfered to make it easier to insert them into the holes. The pegs should have vertical grooves along the sides to allow excess glue to escape when the peg is driven into the hole.

Most woodworkers make their own pegs out of lengths of dowel. The most common size is 9mm diameter and is used for most furniture construction.

To make dowel pegs cut off the required lengths of dowel and round the ends slightly with glasspaper or a file. To allow the glue to escape make a shallow groove along the length of the dowel by placing a tenon saw upside down in the vice and rubbing the dowel peg carefully back and forth over the blade.

The pegs must fit tightly into the holes, so the diameter of the drill bit must match the dowel exactly. If in doubt about making your own pegs, buy a kit containing dowel pegs and a matching drill bit.

Marking dowel joints Always mark the best face and edge on all the pieces before starting. This is very important in making good joints. All measurements must be from one face or edge only to make the marking on the matching pieces consistent. See page 54 for preparing and marking the timber.

First mark the location of the joint on the vertical piece (called the stile) by holding the pieces together in their final position. Transfer the marks to the edge, then clamp the two pieces together in a vice with the crosspiece or rail in the same location within the marks. Make sure the best sides face outwards.

Mark a line approximately half way across with a marking gauge, working from each face in turn. Finally, draw two lines across with a try-square, spacing them at least 12mm from the edge. Most dowel joints require only two pegs but for greater strength in a stouter framework three pegs may be needed.

Before continuing, mark the hole centres with a centre punch or a nail point as a guide for the drill.

Drilling the dowel joint The holes can be drilled with a brace and auger bit but it is much easier to use an electric drill. Use ordinary twist drill bits or buy special wood dowel bits.

There are three points to keep in mind when drilling the holes.

1. The holes must be straight: a dowel peg at an angle will not fit into its matching hole. Stand a try-square nearby when you are drilling and use it as a guide for holding the drill vertical. Alternatively, you can buy a special dowel-drilling jig which clamps on to the wood to guide the drill in vertically.

2. The holes must be the correct diameter. Test the drill size by tapping a peg into a hole drilled in a piece of scrap wood. It should be tight enough to require tapping in with a mallet or hammer, but not so tight that it splits the wood. Use another drill bit if it is too large or too small.

3. The holes should be drilled to approximately the same depth so that the dowels will extend equally into the two members. Make the holes about 3mm deeper than half the length of the dowel pegs. There are several ways of making a marker or depth stop to fit on to the drill bit to obtain all the holes of the same depth. The simplest is to wrap a piece of masking tape around the drill bit to mark the depth to which you want it to go into the wood. A depth stop can be made by drilling through a piece of 25mm × 25mm softwood to the full length of the drill bit, then cut off however much is required to fit over the drill bit: the distance the drill bit sticks out will be the depth of the holes. Keep the depth stops you make and mark the depth on them for use on other jobs. Most manufacturers sell a stop that can be attached to an electric drill and adjusted to the required length.

Before unclamping the pieces it is a good idea to countersink the holes slightly to locate the dowel peg during assembly.

Assembling the dowel joint Always fit the pegs to the end of the cross piece first. Add a dab of woodworking glue to the hole, then tap the dowel peg in, preferably with a wooden mallet, or use a hammer and a block of wood if a mallet is not available. Add glue to the holes in the vertical piece and assemble the joint. Leave the glue to set before any more work is carried out on the joint.

One advantage of dowel joints is that they usually do not require clamping together. If the dowels fit correctly the two pieces can be tapped together to form a tight joint. Tap dowel pegs into a plank of wood for an ingenious coat rack.

To make a dowel joint clamp the timber in the vice and mark the position of the holes to be drilled through both pieces with a try-square and marking gauge **(1)**, *then* **(2)** *punch the hole centres and finally* **(3)** *drill the holes for the dowel pegs in each piece.*

BELOW: *The assembled dowel joint shows the best face and side marked with a pencilled loop. The dowel peg has been grooved with a saw to contain the excess glue and rounded at the end to slot comfortably into the hole.*

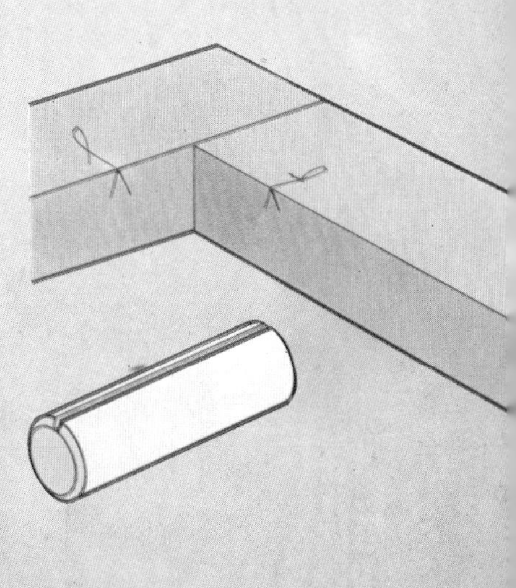

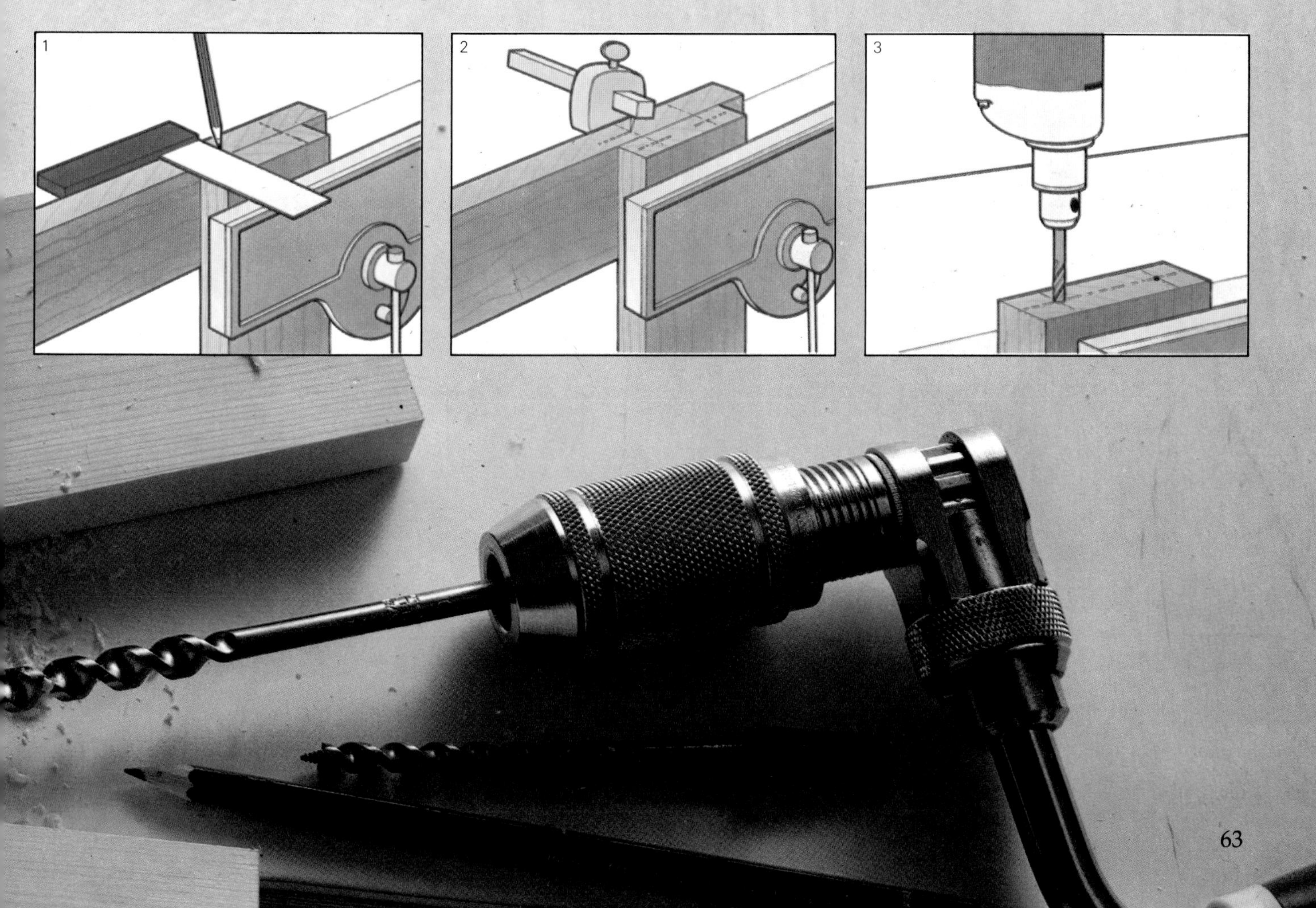

Project: Making a dishrack

Mark and cut the 25 × 50mm into two equal 460mm lengths. (See page 54 for instructions on marking and cutting.) Clean up the sawn ends by sanding or planing. Round the edges and ends with medium and then fine glasspaper.

Cut off 20 pieces of dowel, 150mm long, and sand one end on each.

To mark the holes for the drilling, first mark one piece with 9 light pencil lines 50mm apart, starting 30mm in from one end. Clamp the pieces together and transfer the lines across both pieces with a pencil and try-square.

Mark the hole centres with a marking gauge or by drawing a line with a ruler down the centre.

Finally, mark the holes for the two connecting dowels by turning the two pieces on edge and drawing a line across at each end, 55mm in from the edge.

Before drilling, mark the centres with a centre punch or a nail point. Drill first the four holes for the connecting dowels in the edges to a depth of about 30mm using a depth stop if possible.

Drill the other 18 holes straight through: drill part way through from one side until the drill point just shows through, then turn the piece over and finish the hole from the other side, to avoid the wood cracking or splitting.

Glue the dowels into their holes, and clean off any excess glue with a damp rag. When set, apply three coats matt or gloss varnish.

Dishrack

Things to buy:

- 1m of 25 × 50mm softwood, such as pine
- Approximately 3.3m of 12mm dowel
- Woodworking glue
- Polyurethane varnish (matt or gloss)

Tools needed

- Electric drill or hand-brace
- 12mm drill bit
- Try-square
- Pencil
- Centre punch (or nail)
- Small saw (tenon saw)
- Bench hook (see page 23)
- Glasspaper (medium and fine)

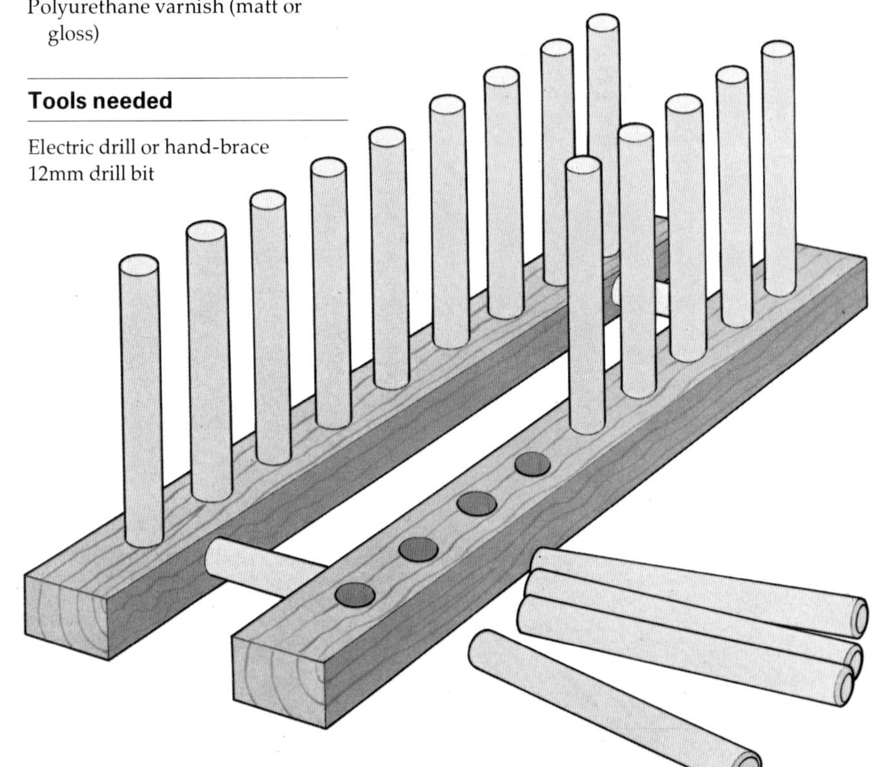

LEFT: *For the dishrack to be successful, the holes where the pegs are inserted must be marked properly so that both rows align exactly. As an alternative to a plate rack, this construction could be made for keeping letters tidy.*

Using dowel joints

Dowel joints are often used in industry to join pieces of wood together. They are not only used for ordinary timber but also very frequently to join sheet materials like plywood, blockboard and especially chipboard.

Corner joints Dowel joints make stronger corner joints than halving joints. Usually they are used to make a rectangular frame with two verticals (stiles) and two cross pieces (rails).

This type of framework is frequently used for making the sides and doors of cabinets. It is also often used to connect the legs and rails of tables.

To make a simple table, using dowel joints, make legs either square or rectangular, say about 50 × 75mm. Make the rails, which can be slightly thinner, (about 25 × 75mm) and dowel joint the legs to the rails with two 9mm diameter dowels for each joint.

Make a simple and attractive table top from a piece of plywood or blockboard veneered with oak or mahogany or painted with gloss paint. Cover the edges of the plywood either with a matching iron-on veneer edging or with a thin strip of moulding glued and nailed on to cover the edges. Set the nails and fill the holes for a smooth finished surface.

Edge joints Another frequent use of dowels is for edge-to-edge joints where, for example, a number of narrow boards are to be glued together to make up a table top. These are marked out and drilled in the same way as with other dowel joints by clamping them together face sides out and squaring lines across. The short dowel pegs serve two functions. They strengthen the joint and keep the boards from slipping up or down when the boards are being clamped together.

Use boards which are at least 22mm thick and insert dowels approximately every 400mm, placing one near each end. Glue not only the dowels but also the edges of the boards. When assembling, clamp them up fairly tightly. After the glue has set, plane off the surface slightly using a long plane, and trim the ends to size.

T-Joints Dowel T-joints are made exactly the same was as corner joints, and are also commonly used in furniture making. One interesting way to make shelves is to connect the shelf to the vertical support using 2 dowels. It is much easier to let the shelf rest on the dowel pegs than to drill holes directly into the shelf. In this way, by drilling matching holes all the way up the insides of the uprights, it is very easy to move the pegs from hole to hole to adjust the height of the shelves as required.

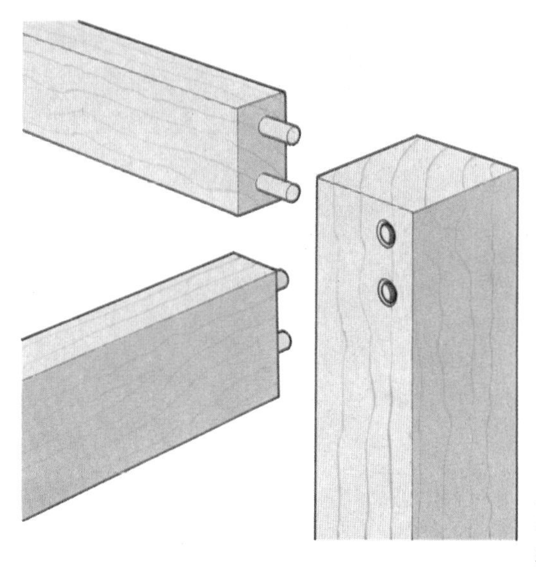

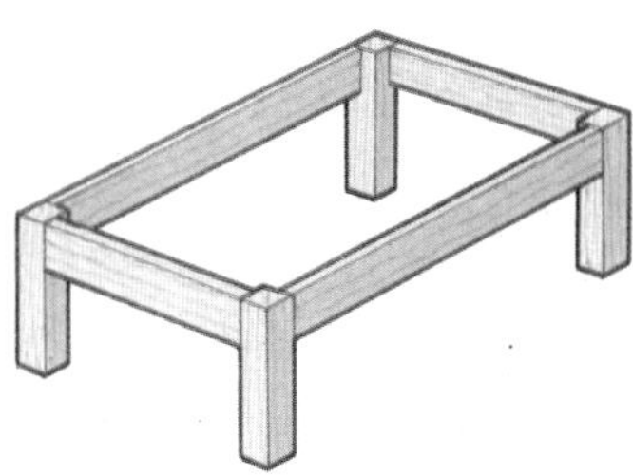

ABOVE: *The construction of the coffee table shown is based upon the dowel joint which has been used to secure the legs to the frame (see* **left***).*

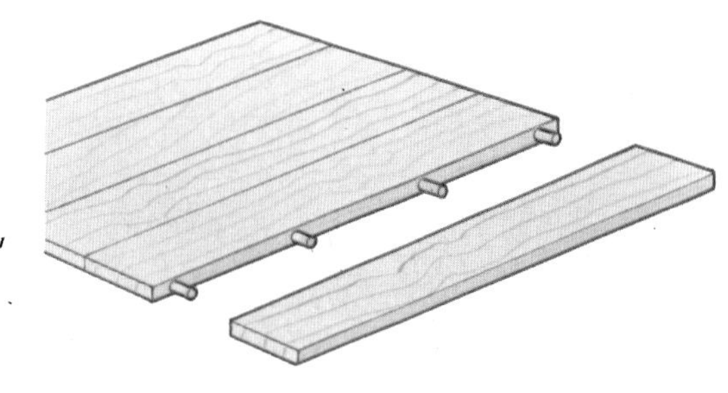

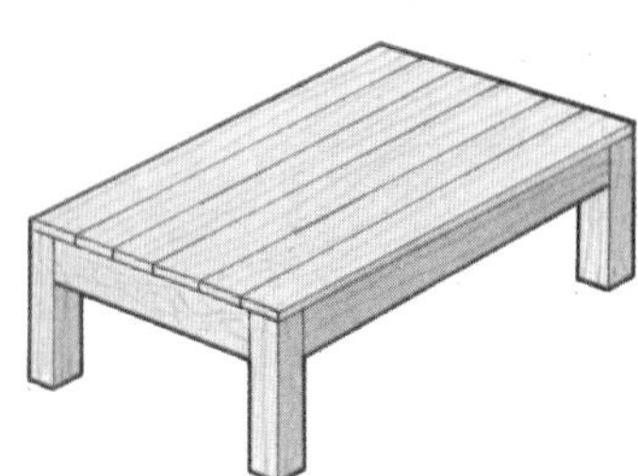

Dowel joints are also used for joining timber into continuous surfaces such as this table top. This type of joint is efficient for both strength and correct alignment of edges.

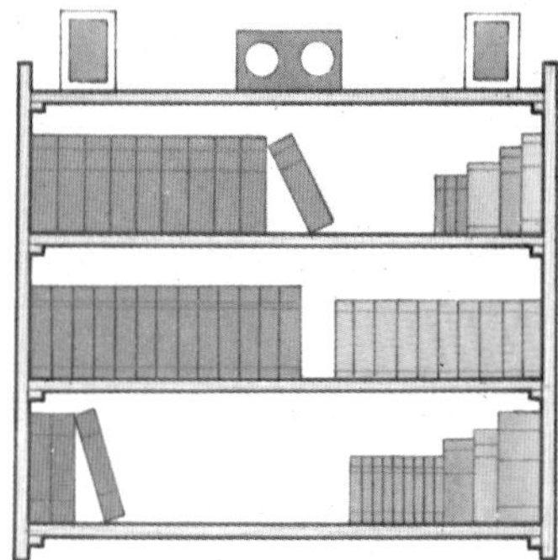

Dowel pegs provide useful supports for adjustable shelves and even when nothing is placed on top still look attractive. By drilling sets of holes at regular intervals, you can move the shelves to the desired height and rest them on dowels.

Mitre joints

Mitre joints are corner joints made by cutting both pieces at exactly 45° so that they fit together squarely.

They are used most often for making picture frames: the mitre is glued and reinforced with a thin nail from each side.

Mitre joints are not as strong as halving or dowel corner joints and are therefore not used for any heavy frames. But they are frequently used at the corners of cabinet doors, where a neat 45° line at the corner looks more elegant and finished than a square dowel joint. These mitres are usually reinforced with hidden dowel pegs to give them extra strength.

Using a mitre box To make a mitre joint it is essential to have some means of cutting the board or moulding at an exact 45° angle. Frame-makers use a guillotine-like machine which cuts the mouldings at 45° with one press of a foot pedal. The easiest way to cut a 45° angle at home is to use an inexpensive mitre-box as a guide for the tenon saw. Use as fine a saw as possible; the more teeth it has the finer the cut will be.

Before using the mitre box, screw a longer

piece of wood, of, say, 12mm plywood on to the base, extending it about 250mm on either side. This serves to support the end of the moulding when cutting and also protects the base from cut marks. Replace it or move it over slightly when the sawmarks become too deep.

Cutting the mitre is not difficult. The only difficulty is marking the pieces correctly so that the opposite sides of the frame are exactly the same length; if they are slightly different there will be a gap at one of the corners.

Cut the first mitre, using even, steady strokes without forcing the saw. Mark the length required and replace the moulding in the mitre box. A useful hint is to make a mark or clamp a block at the cut end, to form a stop from which the other piece can be cut to exactly the same length.

The most common mistake in cutting mitres is to cut the second 45° angle the wrong way. It happens to everyone. Remember that the angles all point toward the centre of the frame when it is put together.

Assembling the mitre joint After cutting the mitres on the two pairs of moulding, one pair for the sides and one pair for the top and bottom, clean off the ends carefully with a piece of fine glasspaper on a sanding block or piece of wood. Be careful not to round the edges, just sand carefully with a few strokes along the 45° angle.

Start assembling at one corner. Before joining the mitres together, drill a small hole in the end for a reinforcing panel pin, add glue to the two sides and put them together, waiting to tap in the panel pins after the glue has set.

Continue with the other three joints. The frame will not be rigid until all the joints are assembled and the glue has set.

To hold the frame together until the glue sets use special mitre clamps or, more simply, tie a piece of heavy string tightly around the frame, (see page 34).

For heavier frames such as cabinet doors use longer panel pins, several each side, or use dowel pegs to strengthen the joint.

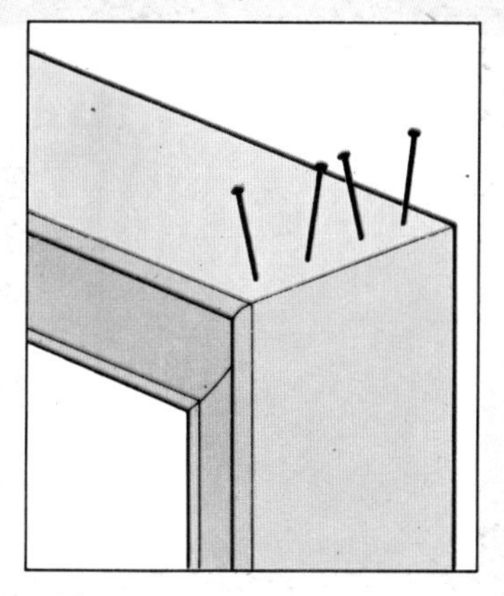

To make a mitre joint stronger, nail in panel pins along the joint. Drive them in slightly skew in opposing directions (as shown) for the most effective grip.

BELOW: *Mitre cramps are commonly used to hold picture frames while the glue sets.*

Picture frame

Things to buy:

- 1.7m of gold hockey stick moulding
- A few panel pins, 19mm long
- Woodworking glue
- A piece of 2mm thick glass, cut to size by your glass merchant
- A piece of heavy cardboard backing
- A piece of mounting board, colour to complement the picture
- A piece of hanging wire and two hooks

Tools needed:

- A fine saw (tenon saw)
- Mitre box
- Pin hammer
- Hand drill with drill bit
- Sanding block with fine glasspaper
- A piece of heavy string or mitre clamps

Project: Making a picture frame

Picture frame moulding is available at local do-it-yourself shops. There is a wide variety of mouldings available, in various shapes and sizes. The one used here is hockey stick. Choose one to complement your picture.

This frame is 320mm × 380mm. To make a larger or smaller frame plan out the lengths of moulding and sizes of backing required.

Measure the picture and plan out how much mounting board, if used, should show around the picture, and work out the final size of the frame. It helps to draw a picture of the frame, full size if necessary, with the dimensions of the components shown clearly for reference.

The glass, picture and boards all fit into the rectangular slot in the moulding called the rebate. In this way the edges of the boards and glass are hidden and held securely. Keep this in mind when planning the size of the frame. It is best to make the frame first to the size required, and to cut the mounting and the backing boards afterwards to fit the actual frame. This ensures a much better fit.

Cut the four moulding pieces and assemble the frame, gluing and nailing the mitred corners. Clamp the frame together with the piece of string until the glue has dried.

Finally, after making the frame, have the glass cut to the correct size, minus a millimetre in both directions, by the glass merchant.

Cut an opening in the mounting board with a very sharp trimming knife (use a new blade) to leave a window for the picture.

Insert the glass, mounting board, picture and backing and hold them in place with a few pins or with special tacks, available from do-it-yourself shops.

Finally, screw the two hooks on the back, one on either side of the moulding about a third of the way down. String the wire from one to the other and hang the picture.

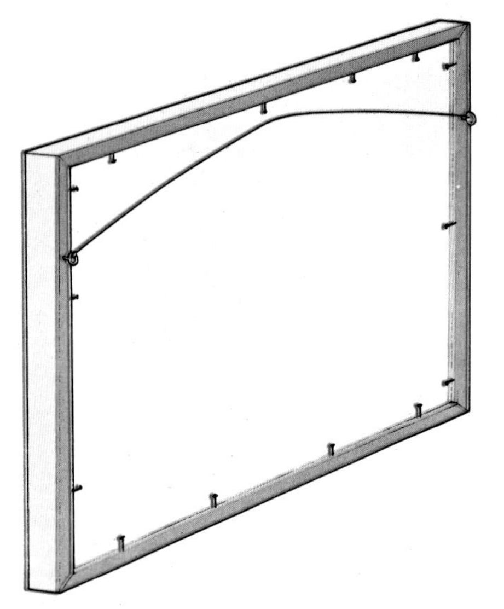

ABOVE: *Looking at the picture frame from the back, the components are the glass front* **(1)**, *the mounting board for the picture* **(2)**, *the picture itself* **(3)** *and the cardboard backing piece* **(4)**.

LEFT: *The back piece is held in place by panel pins tapped in around the edge of the frame.*

Using mitre joints

Mitre joints are used mainly to make picture frames and doors.

The method of reinforcing the corners varies according to the use and thickness of the frames.

The most common method for picture frames is to pin the corners with panel pins which can be sunk flush with or below the surface. For small frames use one pin each side but for larger ones use more, slanting them in opposite directions for a firmer grip.

A mitre joint reinforced with dowel pegs is much stronger but also quite difficult to do accurately.

An easier way to reinforce the joint is to make a series of fine saw cuts across the mitre after the glue has set. Glue thin strips of wood veneer of the same material as the frame into the grooves, and trim off the waste carefully with a block plane after the glue has set.

Heavy frames for cabinet or cupboard doors can also be dowelled from the outside to reinforce the mitre joints. Use timber approximately 20mm thick and 75mm wide, though it can, of course, be made lighter or heavier depending on the size and use of the door.

After assembling the frame, add perhaps one nail in each corner just to hold the frame together. After the glue has set, hold each corner of the frame in turn in a vice while drilling holes through into the other piece for the dowel pegs. Glue the pegs in place and cut them off flush.

Another versatile use for mitre joints is to apply veneer-edging to the front edges of a cabinet and to mitre the corners. The cabinet can be made of plywood, blockboard or veneered chipboard simply nailed and glued together. To give it a finished look apply the matching veneer edging with an iron, overlapping the corners. Cut through both veneers at a 45° angle with a sharp trimming knife. Put the iron back over the corner to pull away the offcuts. This gives the piece a handsome finish and is frequently used on veneered pieces like radio and TV cabinets.

Picture frames are expensive to buy and even more expensive to have made by a professional framer. To make them yourself, all you need to do is learn how to make mitre joints and then you can make them very simply. The money you save will enable you to go to the higher-priced frames, although very often the simplest pine frames are the most effective; it very much depends upon the object being framed.

Mechanical joints

Every piece of furniture contains nails, screws or some form of hardware. In modern furniture, screws and other fittings are often left exposed as a design feature where they can look very effective if carefully positioned.

Sometimes it is much easier and quicker to nail or screw two pieces of wood together than to mark and cut out, say, a halving joint; and mechanical fixings can be just as strong and stable as woodworking joints.

The decision to use a mechanical fixing depends on several factors, such as how much time you want to spend on a project and how fine a piece it is. A crossbrace for the shed door, for example, should be nailed or screwed, whereas the corner joint of a cabinet door should be dowelled or mitred for a professional finish.

The joints you decide to make also depend on your skill with tools. For someone who has never used a chisel it is much easier and quicker to nail or screw pieces together.

Nails, screws or other fittings can be used alone or with the traditional joints. They are very quick and convenient and often stronger than the glued wood joints.

There are so many clever and attractive fittings on the market that it is quite often better to use mechanical fixings than to make complex woodworking joints. This is especially true when working with sheet materials. A plastic block joint, for example, is an ingenious device which makes it very easy to join two panels of chipboard or blockboard together.

Nailed joints

Nailed joints are most often used for temporary projects and in construction work. For furniture and other smaller projects, nailed joints used in conjunction with glue can be very strong. Panel pins which have a small head can be sunk below the surface of the wood for a hidden fixing. See the table of available nails and sizes on page 52 before choosing the nail for the job.

Nailing wood The size of the nail to be used depends on the size of wood. Always nail the smaller or thinner piece to the larger or thicker one. Choose a nail which will penetrate as far as possible into the bottom piece without going through the other side. Where the final look of the work is not a consideration, as in some

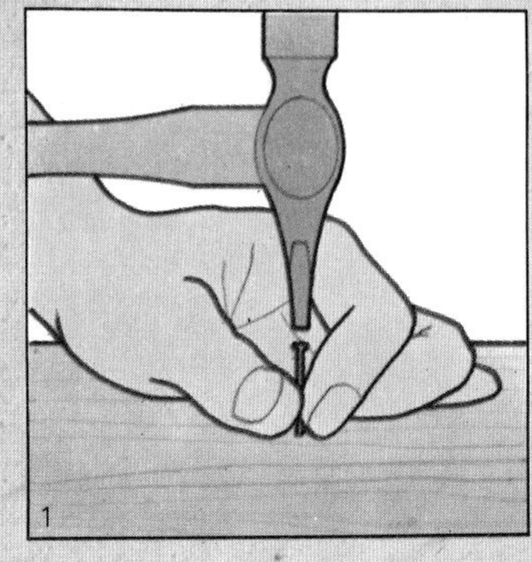

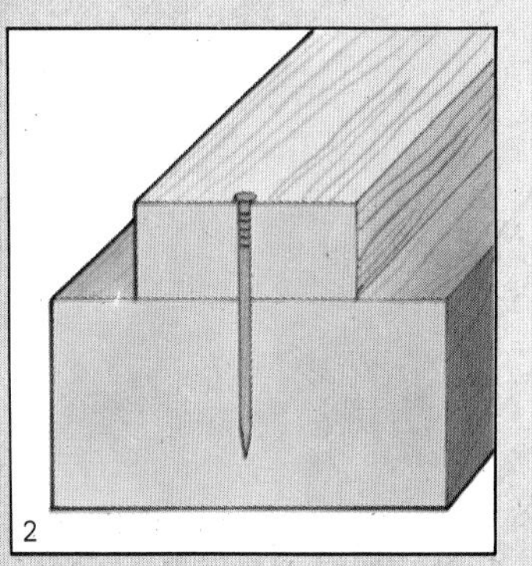

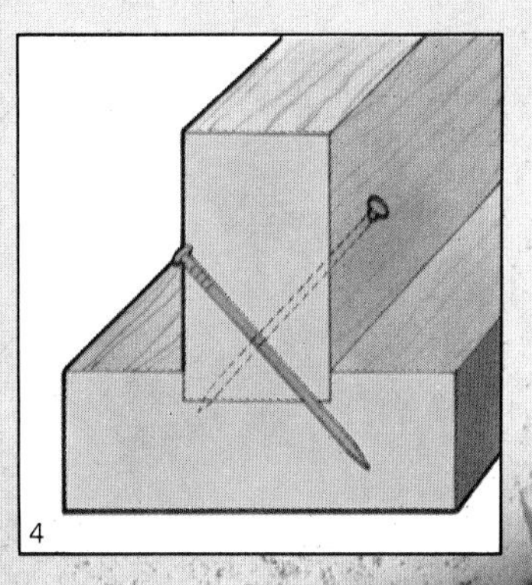

1 *For hammering a small nail, use the cross-pein end of a pin hammer.*
2 *Always choose a nail that is long enough to go through one piece of timber and at least half-way into the piece to which it is being joined.*
3 *Nail through the thinner piece first. On work where the fixings will not show, you can bend nails over to give the join a firmer hold.*
4 *Skew nailing allows you to drive a nail into awkward corners.*

construction work, drive the nail straight through both pieces, then bend the ends over into the wood. This makes the connection extremely strong.

If the nail is too large or is nailed too near the end of a board, the wood may split. To avoid splitting, use finer nails or panel pins. For some hardwoods or brittle woods which split easily it may be necessary to drill holes slightly smaller than the nails to prevent splitting the wood when hammering in the nail.

One method to strengthen a joint is skew nailing, that is, hammering nails in at an angle. Where possible, nail every other nail at an alternate angle.

Smaller nails and panel pins tend to bend more easily than heavy nails. To prevent the nail from bending, support it between your forefinger and thumb until it is part-way in, then use light hammer taps to drive it in.

To drive in very small pins, use the cross-pin end of the pin hammer, with the pin heads supported between your fingers. Alternatively, push the nail through a piece of cardboard which is easy to hold while tapping in the pin.

OPPOSITE: *This attractive sewing box is simply softwood nailed together with the nail heads set below the surface of the wood so that they can be filled and sanded smooth. The nailed joints are not at all visible because of the care taken in sinking the nails and sanding the filler when it dried.*

Project: Making a small sewing box

Cut four pieces of 12 × 75mm for the sides, two pieces 200mm long (A) and two pieces 132mm long (B). Plane the ends smooth if necessary or rub them down with glasspaper.

Nail these pieces together. Start three 19mm panel pins in either end of the 200mm pieces so that the pins just protrude.

Hold one of the shorter (B) pieces in a vice, spread glue over the end and nail on piece A so that the corners are flush. Take it out of the vice, then glue and nail the next piece B. Turn the assembly over and attach the other piece A.

Cut two pieces 200 × 150mm (C), one for the top and one for the bottom, from the 6.5mm plywood piece. Cut a third piece (D), the size of the inside opening of the box. After cutting this piece, try it inside the box for fit. If it does not fit smoothly, shave a little off with the block plane.

Glue and nail the bottom in place using the 12mm nails, about three each side. If the bottom piece is cut correctly, the box will now be square and rigid.

Glue piece D to the middle of the lid so that there is an equal overhang all round. Add a small weight or clamp to keep the two pieces together until the glue sets.

Carry out finishing touches, such as sinking the nails and filling the holes with white wood filler or bevelling the edges of the top and bottom with a block plane, before sanding and covering with one or two coats of clear or wood tone polyurethane.

Before screwing on the knob from underneath, paint the top with two coats of bright red paint, gloss or matt depending on preference. There are, of course, several other variations you can choose for the finish.

Sewing box

Things to buy:

- 700mm of 12 × 75mm softwood such as pine
- One piece of 6.5mm thick plywood, 150 × 600mm
- 12 panel pins 19mm long
- 12 panel pins 12mm long
- One small wooden ball for a knob
- One brass screw 25mm long with cup washer
- Woodworking glue
- White wood filler (optional)
- Polyurethane varnish
- Red paint

Tools needed:

- Tenon saw with bench hook
- Try-square, pencil and ruler
- Pin hammer
- Nail punch
- Block plane (optional)
- Fine glasspaper.

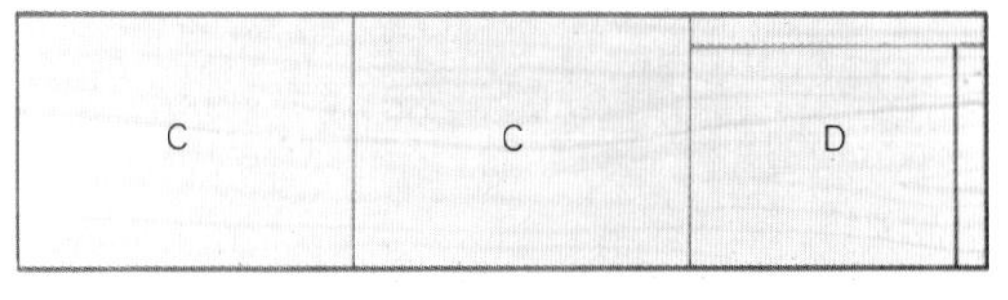

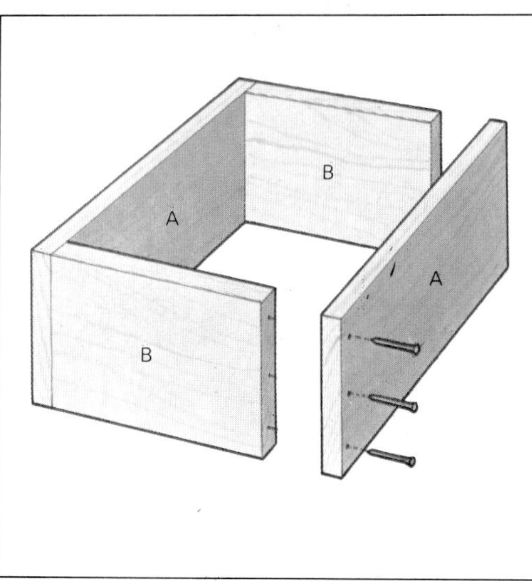

The diagrams show the steps involved in making the box. Nail the two sides to one end and then attach the fourth side the same way. For a decorative touch to the lid, fix a round wooden ball to it by screwing it from underneath. For a different type of effect, you could use a small brass drawer handle instead.

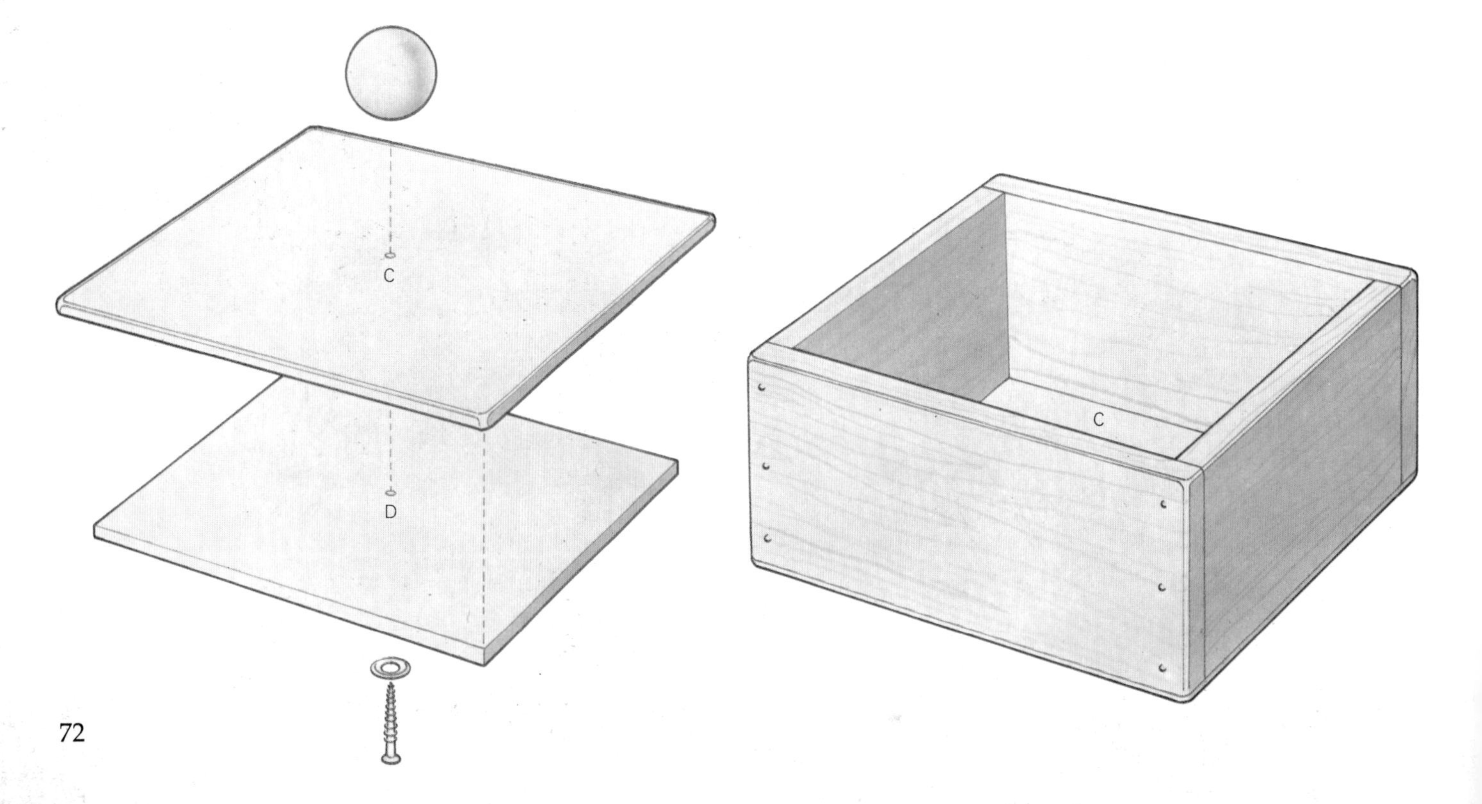

tapisserie wool
49
125
56
142
143
144
57
145
146
58
147
148
59
149
150
151

Nailed joints are used with the timber overlapping as **(1)** *corner or* **(2)** *T- or cross joints. Where no overlapping occurs and the pieces butt up to each other instead, use corrugated fasteners (shown in* **3***) for a quick fixing.*

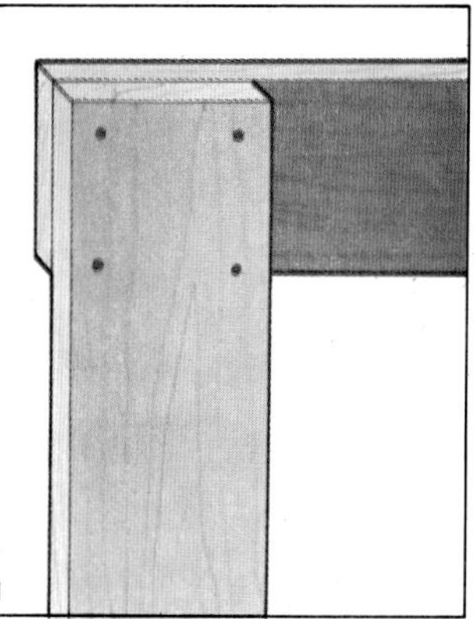

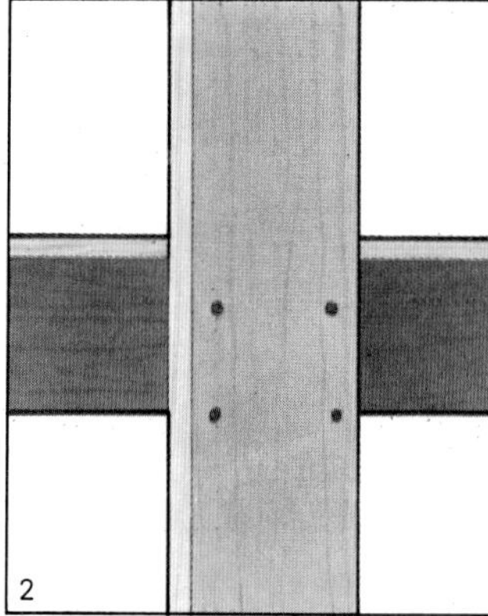

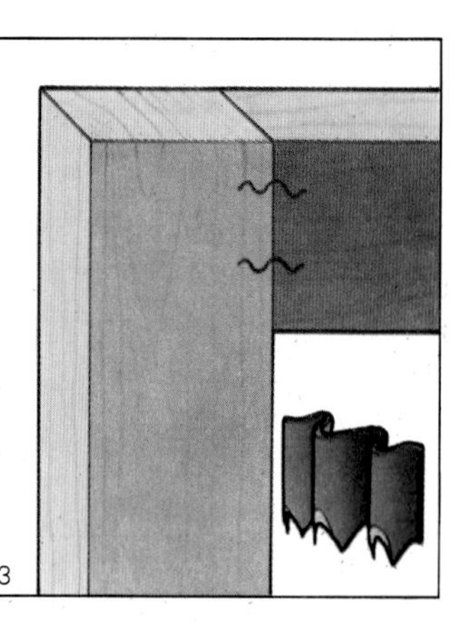

BELOW: *These simple step-ups can be made with plywood or timber. Nailed-and-glued joints are the basis of their construction.*

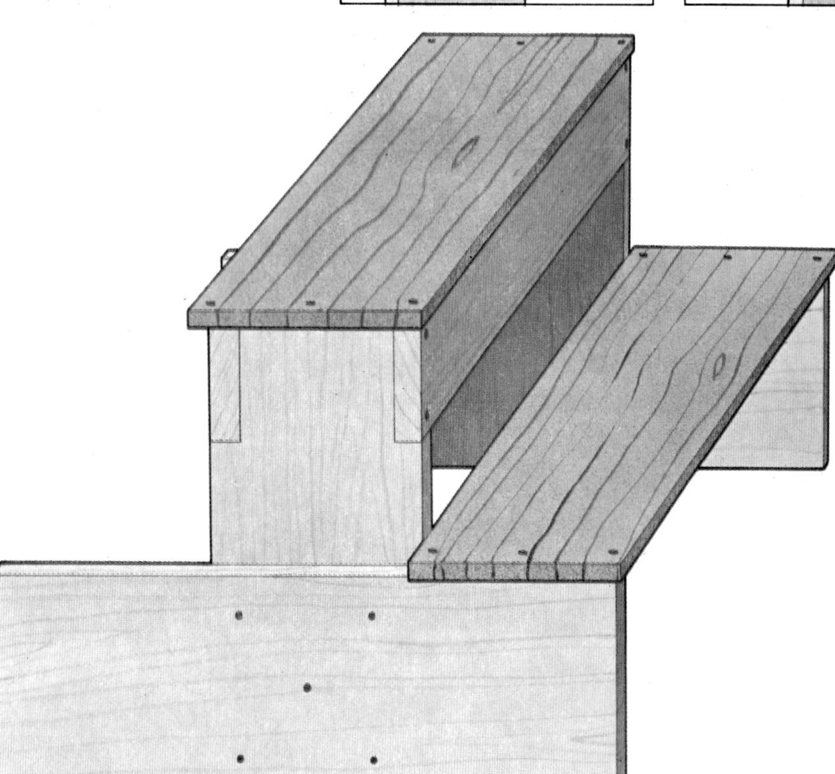

Using nailed joints

Nails are used in a variety of joints to connect not only timber but also plywood and chipboard panels.

For extra strength it is advisable to apply glue to the joint, unless the pieces will have to be taken apart later.

Cross joints and T-joints Nailed cross and T-joints can simply be overlapped or they can be made as halving joints, described on page 58. To make the joint rigid, add at least three nails spaced around the joint. Avoid nailing too near the edge or the wood will split.

Nailed T-joints are often useful in connecting two wide boards, as for this simple trestle. To make the trestles use plywood pieces at least 150mm wide with about six nails per joint, and add glue for extra strength. The pair of trestles should be made to a comfortable height, about 600mm, to be used to support a decorating table, as step ladders, or even to support a worktop.

Corner joints Nailed corner joints in softwood often need reinforcing with small battens, because the nails tend to split the end of the board.

Plywood does not split as easily because of the layers of cross plies, so nailed corner joints in plywood used for boxes or small drawers are usually quite strong.

Corner joints with the timber lying flat, as for a frame, should not be nailed because nails have no holding power in end grain. An easy substitute for nails are corrugated metal fasteners, which are driven in with a hammer and hold both pieces quite firmly together.

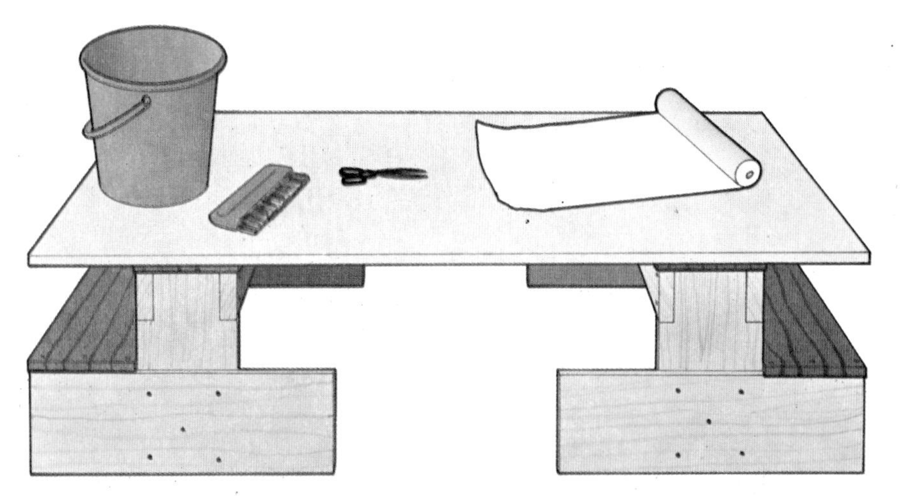

LEFT: *The step-ups form an excellent support for a decorating table. Space them apart as required and lay a sheet of plywood or timber on top. The step-ups would also be ideal for small children who can not reach a wash basin.*

Screwed joints

Screws are the most widely used mechanical fixings. They are also used to reinforce traditional glued joints. When in doubt about how to connect a joint, use screws; properly fastened, they make extremely strong and durable joints.

For most work, use countersunk steel screws, or the more expensive brass screws if rusting or appearance is a consideration. Countersunk screws fit flush with the surface. The head fits into a hole made with a countersink bit on a drill. All screws require drilled holes, as they cannot be driven directly into the wood like nails.

Attaching screws requires much more care than hammering nails. Choose the length so that the screw extends into the bottom piece by at least half the screw length, but not so long that it pokes through the other side. It is usually best to hold the screw up to the two pieces to be joined to check its length.

Mark the screw locations before drilling a clearance hole, the same diameter as the shank of the screw, to about half the depth, and drill the bottom half of the hole with a drill bit which is smaller than the threads. In softwoods it is often convenient to drill one small hole only, but in hardwoods always drill both holes carefully.

You can usually estimate the depth of the hole by eye, but where accuracy is critical, for example when drilling in the underside of a table top, it is best to use a simple depth stop made from a short length of dowel or a 25 × 25mm batten which has been cut off to the required length.

For smaller screws up to about 19mm long you can use a bradawl to make a clearance hole in softwoods. Start the blade of the bradawl across the grain then make a hole by rotating the bradawl back and forth.

Use at least two screws per joint, spacing the screw positions out evenly and marking the positions clearly for drilling and clearance holes. When it is difficult to hold the pieces together and handle the tools at the same time, clamp the pieces together until the holes are drilled and the screws inserted.

As with nailed joints, glue strengthens a screwed joint but is only important where the screws may not be sufficiently strong by themselves. If the correct size screw is not available, a slightly shorter screw can be used and the joint strengthened with glue.

Screws are also used to attach most hardware such as hinges, locks, and drawer pulls to wood. Hold the piece of hardware in position and mark the hole locations with a pencil or a marking awl, which has a fine point especially for marking the centres of holes. Most hardware has countersunk holes which require exactly the right screw size for a correct fit.

Screw-collars fitted under the counter-sunk heads give the screw heads a finished look and the screws do not need to be countersunk. Screw collars are generally available in chrome and brass finishes for Nos. 4, 6, 8 and 10 screws.

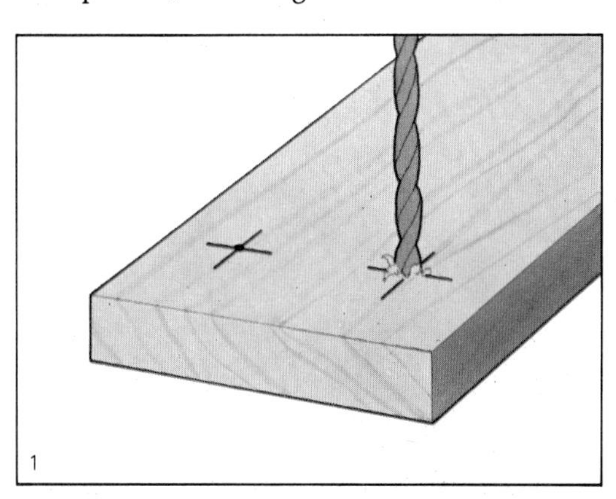

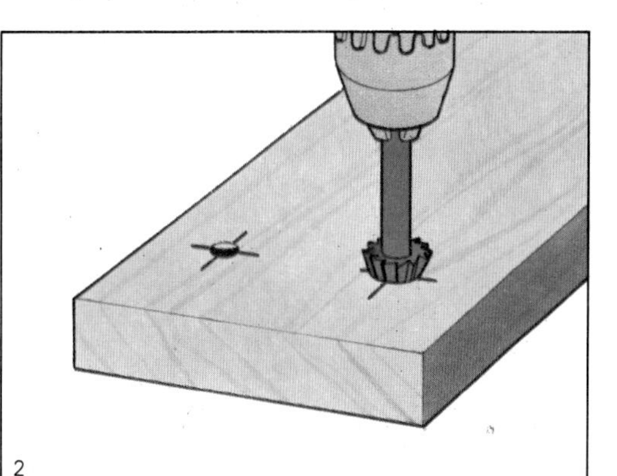

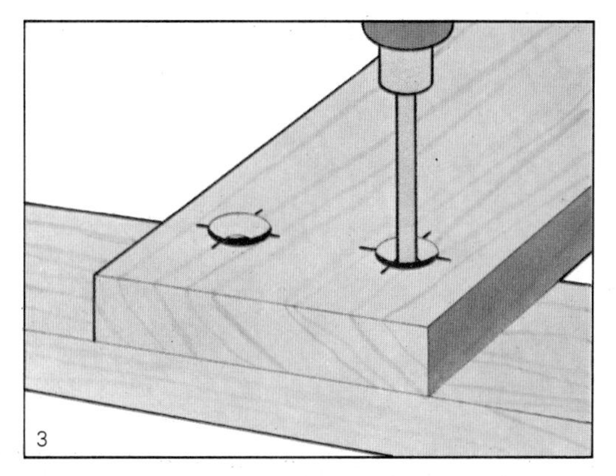

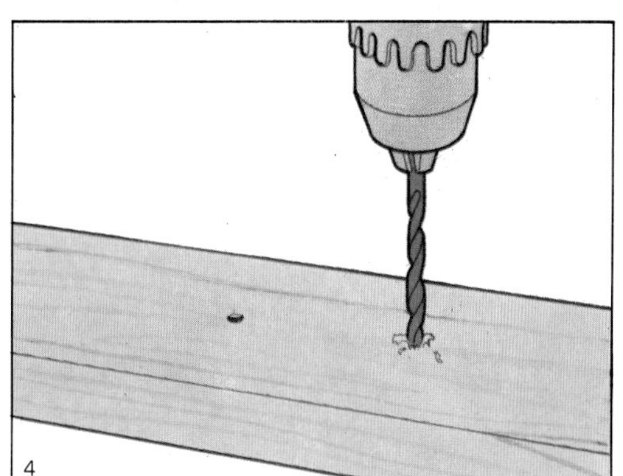

For a professionally made screwed joint first drill a clearance hole to about half the depth of the screw using a bit the same diameter as that of the screw, then complete the bottom half with a slightly narrower bit. ***1*** *Mark and punch the centres for the holes before drilling the first half of the clearance hole.* ***2*** *A countersink bit forms a conical hole at the top so that when the screw is inserted it will be flush with the surface.* ***3*** *To make sure that the boards align when they are screwed together you need to match the bottom board with the drilled top piece. When the position has been checked, insert an awl or nail through the top clearance hole to mark the drilling hole for the bottom.* ***4*** *For smaller screws drill a clearance hole with a narrow bit, as shown, or a bradawl.*

Hansel and Gretel
NUTSHELL LIBRARY
by MAURICE SENDAK
PIERRE
COLLINS

Project: Making a shelf unit

Cut the 25 × 75mm board into five pieces, for three shelves 450mm long and two uprights 345mm long.

Mark the shelf locations on the insides of both verticals. Measure and mark on one, hold them together and transfer the marks across with a try square.

Mark two lines 20mm in from the edge along each upright. Drill holes along this line in the centre of each shelf location. Drill the holes straight through.

Before attaching shelves paint all the pieces with two coats of bright red gloss or satin paint. Alternatively leave the unit natural and apply two coats of clear polyurethane.

Hold a shelf firmly along the marks and mark the two hole locations on the end of the shelf. Drill the same diameter holes to a depth of about 25mm in the ends of the shelf.

Insert a fibre wall plug into the end of each hole and attach the shelf by screwing through the upright into the fibre wall plug with a screw collar fitted around each screw.

Normally screws driven into the end grain of wood, as for these shelves, would not hold very well, but by using fibre wall plugs the screws hold by friction and not by the thread.

Finally, attach the mirror brackets to the top shelf on the other end and screw the shelf unit to the wall with No. 10 round-headed brass screws at least 32mm long.

BELOW: *Simply mark the position of the shelves on the inside of the side supports, as shown* **far left**, *and measure the shelves to fit between. For hanging the unit on the wall, you can use simple mirror brackets such as the ones shown.*

Shelf unit

Things to buy:

Approximately 2m of 25 × 75mm softwood
12 No. 8 brass countersunk screws, 38mm long
12 No. 8 brass screw cups
12 No. 8 fibre wall plugs, 19mm long
Two brass mirror brackets with matching 12mm screws
Paint or polyurethane

Tools needed:

Try square and pencil
Ruler
Tenon saw
Drill with 4.5mm drill bit
Hammer
Screwdriver
Paintbrush

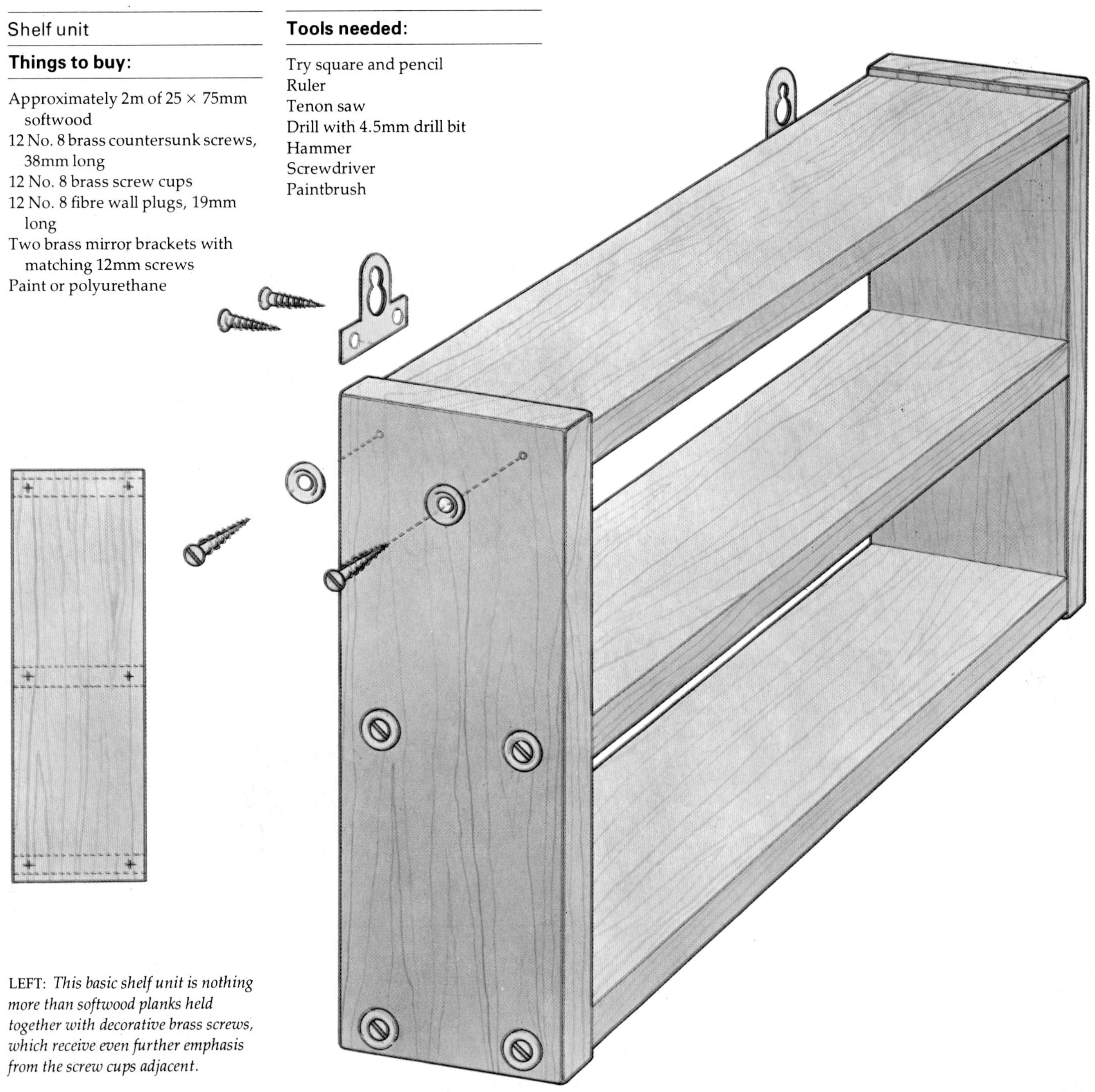

LEFT: *This basic shelf unit is nothing more than softwood planks held together with decorative brass screws, which receive even further emphasis from the screw cups adjacent.*

Using screwed joints

Screws are used to make or strengthen almost every kind of woodworking joint. They are particularly useful in connecting plywood and blockboard. For chipboard, special chipboard screws with coarser thread are used, which are either screwed directly in the chipboard or into special plastic connectors.

T-joints Screws generally have no holding power in the end grain of timber, so a batten is required for screwed T-joints. Alternatively insert a wall plug in the clearance hole and screw into that as in the shelf unit above.

The screwed T-joint is particularly useful for putting up simple shelving, either directly on to the wall for, say, an alcove, or on to timber uprights fixed to the wall. Use either 25 × 25mm or 25 × 38mm softwood for battens which are screwed to the uprights. Use 25mm thick softwood boards for shelves up to about 1.2m length. For longer shelves use thicker timber. For wider shelves, use either 19mm thick plywood up to 1m long or use 25mm thick Parana pine boards in widths up to 300mm.

The shelves can either be screwed down with a couple of small screws or can simply rest on the battens, as shown on the drawing below.

Corner joints For overlapping boards use two or three screws per joint and for boards or plywood butted together use a batten to reinforce the joint.

This type of screwed corner joint is particularly useful in making boxes such as a toy bin on castors: usc 12mm plywood sides with a 6.5mm plywood bottom screwed in place. Attach castors to each corner, then paint in bright colours and add lettering or attractive transfers. Screw on knobs for handles or drill 25mm diameter finger holes. This toy box can be adapted to become a seat; simply add a lid and cover it with a cushion.

Cross lap joint For two boards lying across one another it is extremely easy to add two or three screws to make a solid joint. Make sure the pieces are square before drilling the holes and attaching the screws. Two temporary nails help to position the boards correctly.

A very simple table can be made using screwed cross joints. Use 25 × 75mm softwood, hardwood or plywood for all the rails and legs, screw them together with brass or chrome screws with screw cups as a decorative touch, and simply lay the plywood or blockboard top in place to finish.

Corners are easy to make as long as you use the correct technique. When the pieces overlap **(1)** *use a T-joint; when they butt together* **(2)** *insert a small batten between for anchoring the screws. The toybox illustrates the second technique whereas the book shelves are simple overlapped joints whereby the shelves are screwed to the battens on which they rest. Note the placement of the screws* **(right)** *for the two types of construction.*

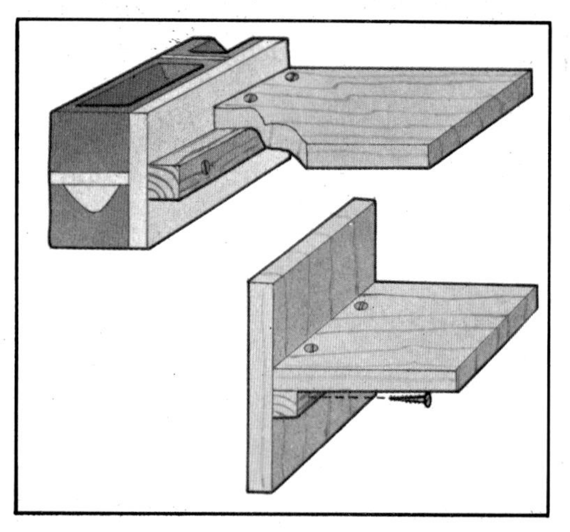

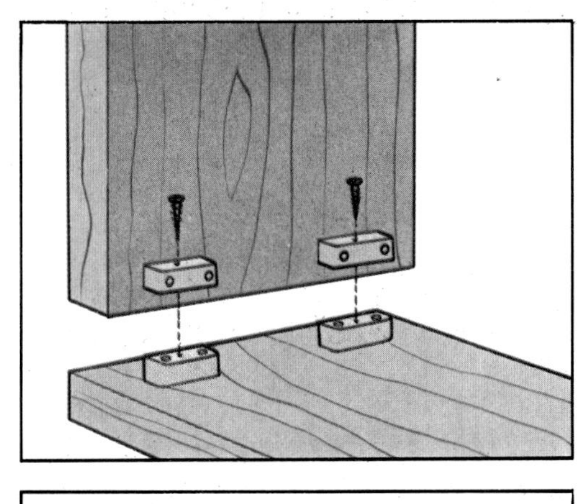

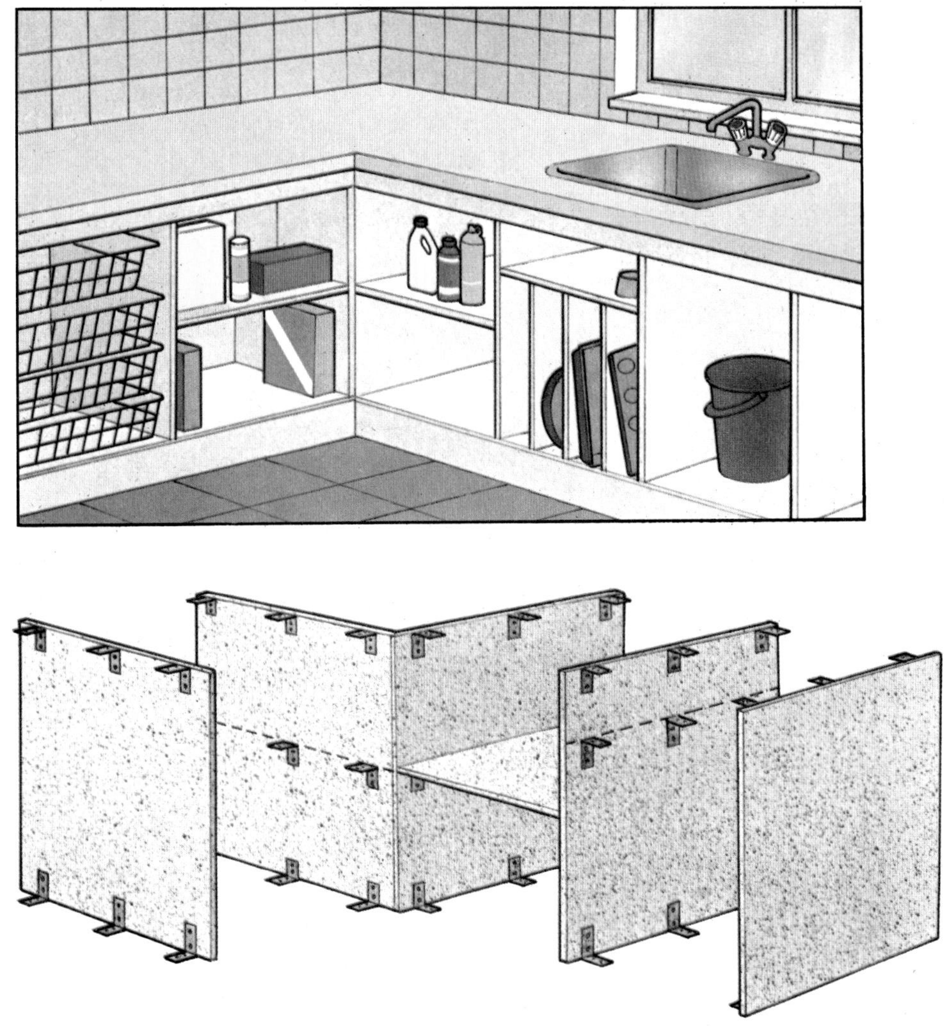

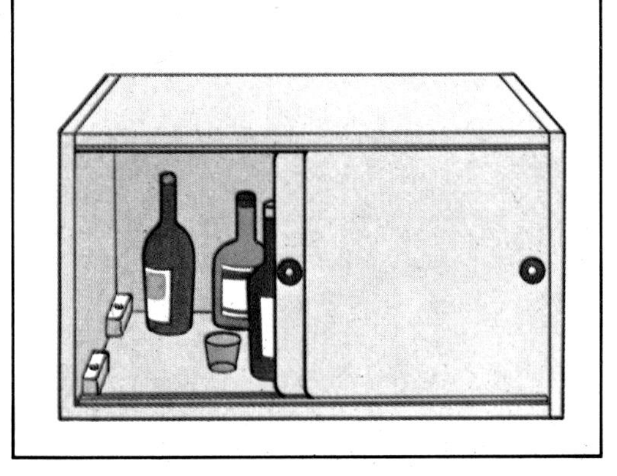

Where extra strength is required, as in shelves built for holding fairly heavy materials, use plastic block joints (top left) to connect the timber or sheet materials (see drinks cabinet), or less modern but equally efficient metal brackets (bottom right). The kitchen units (above right) are held together by a network of 90-degree metal brackets. The diagram (right) shows how neat this method can be.

Joints with special fittings With the increased use of knock-down construction in modern furniture, new fittings have been developed which make the joining of wood especially easy. Many of these are available only through the furniture trade but some can be bought at local do-it-yourself shops.

The block joint, for example, consists of two plastic halves which bolt together. They are used, two per joint, to make corner or T-joints in panels, particularly those made of chipboard.

Each half is screwed to one of the panels. The joints are completed as the panels are brought together and the two halves bolted tight.

Block joints enable cabinets and wall units to be made very easily out of sheet material panels. For a simple, wall-hung drinks cabinet, for example, use white melamine covered chipboard, available in 2.44m long panels in various widths. Use white block joints to connect the corners, and cover any sawn edges with white plastic iron-on edging. Make the cabinet about 350mm high and 750mm wide. Simple sliding doors made from 3mm thick white hardboard slide in plastic tracks simply glued in place.

Metal plates are not a new invention but they are nonetheless extremely useful to connect timber or sheet materials. There are three basic shapes available in various sizes. They are connected to the wood with countersunk screws. Determine the size of screws to use by trying them in the holes. 19mm long screws are usually adequate but in some cases longer screws may be required.

Using the angle to connect panels together, a simple kitchen cabinet can be made from plywood, blockboard or chipboard. For the verticals attach the bottom edge to the floor with two brackets. The horizontal dividers are attached to the uprights with two angles on either end. The 19mm chipboard top is also attached with metal brackets. It is then covered by gluing down a plastic laminate. See page 82 for covering the edge with strippings or mouldings.

It is easy to add more shelves or perhaps pull-out wire baskets for tins and vegetables. These baskets, available at large department stores or through hobby magazines, slide on metal runners screwed to the sides.

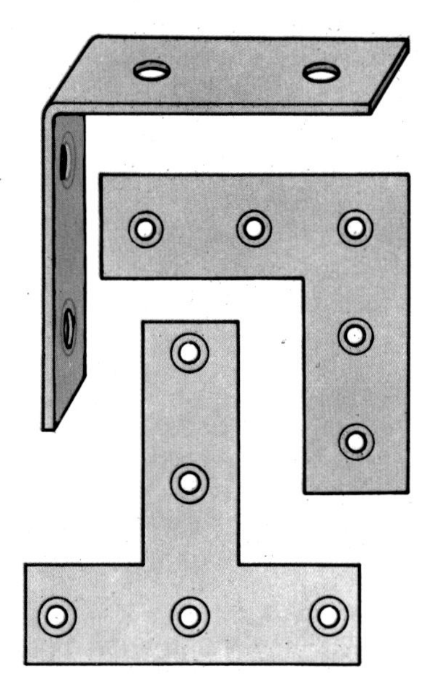

ABOVE: *Metal brackets are available in three basic shapes. In addition to the 90-degree bracket* **(top)**, *brackets can be right-angled and flat-faced for corner reinforcement* **(centre)** *and flat T-shaped* **(bottom)** *for making joints.*

Common mistakes and how to correct them

The impression given in most books on woodworking is that if instructions are followed carefully all the joints will fit together perfectly the first time, frames will be square, nails will go in straight and so on. Anyone who has ever made anything in wood knows this is not so. Professional woodworkers learn to live with the likely mistakes and to correct them as they go along. As each joint is cut it is tried and a bit shaved off here and there to make it fit. When the piece is finally assembled it is usually a matter of trial and error to make everything fit perfectly. A little clamping here and letting out there will usually be like fitting a suit, ending up with a good fit.

Most of the tricks come with long experience of learning from each mistake, but there are several useful hints on correcting mistakes that will come in handy for the beginner.

Wood fillers

There are several types of quick-drying wood fillers. They come in small tins and tubes in a variety of wood shades, but the most common is white or cream for ordinary pine. The inevitable little nicks and blemishes can be filled and sanded off smooth and will hardly be noticed.

With clear finishes on pine, the fillers always show a little, so for especially large cracks it may be better to glue in a fine sliver of wood.

Fillers are especially useful for darker or stained woods and for painted surfaces, which tend to hide the filler better, and for filling the small holes left from setting panel pins or nails below the surface.

The small sewing box on page 73, for example, looks much better if the nail heads do not show: a cream filler to match the pine was used to fill the small holes and produce a much more attractive finish.

Plates and brackets

For all the joints which just will not stay together no matter how much gluing and cramping is carried out, the easiest remedy is to screw on a plate or bracket on the back to hold the joint together. This is useful not only for new projects but also for repairing old pieces of furniture, and there are various shapes of brackets. (See page 34). It is a good idea to have a few of each with matching screws. In making the picture frame on page 69, the main difficulty is in holding the sides together until the glue has set and the nails are added. If it proves insurmountable turn the frame over and screw on a few small, discreet brackets to hold the corners together.

Repairing broken joints

Some wood tends to split quite easily, and many joints break at a weak point while they are being cut or being assembled. Halving joints are very susceptible, especially near the end of the board.

This type of mistake occurs constantly in woodworking and the usual remedy is to glue the piece back on and cramp it until the glue has set. For a small joint it is probably enough to glue the piece back on, but sometimes it is better to strengthen the joint by adding a small screw or dowel peg.

In larger pieces hide the screws completely by counterboring so that the screwhead is at least 10mm below the surface, then plug the hole with a plug of the same wood. Inexpensive plugcutters to be used in an electric drill are available in several diameters. Plugs can be made out of a piece of offcut and glued in the hole to cover the screw. These plugs are so effective that it is often impossible to tell that a hole has been drilled.

Many woodworkers use plugs rather than fillers to remove dents. Fillers draw attention to the flaw if they do not match perfectly. The dent is drilled out with a sharp dowel drill bit, and a plug of the same wood is inserted in the hole and sanded over smoothly.

RIGHT: *The simplest remedy is often all that is required to put right a seemingly intractable mistake. A split halving joint, for example, can be glued and clamped together until it is strong enough for further assembly. Where there are dents or flaws in the wood, or where a hole has been drilled into the wrong place, you can fill such holes with wooden plugs cut with a special drill attachment for this purpose. For wobbly picture frames attach a flat-faced corner plate.*

LEFT: *Reinforce weak corners with metal corner brackets.*

Professional touches

Usually the final touches like rounding off the edges give a job a more professional finished look. Even the plainest looking piece of furniture looks new and interesting with a few of these touches. A table, for example, is usually made from an attractive veneer glued down to chipboard or blockboard. Exposed chipboard edges would look most unattractive, so a wood edge is added to match the veneer and make the table look as if it is made of solid wood.

There are many ways to add these finishing touches to make your projects look professional.

Rounding and bevelling

When the edges and corners of timber or plywood are left square and sharp, the board tends to look slightly clumsy and unfinished. Round the edges with glasspaper, a file, or with a small plane to make the wood look softer and feel nicer to touch. Rounded edges are also safer for children. Table edges, for example, are quite sharp and feel nicer if they are slightly rounded.

Sometimes it is enough to remove the sharp edge with glasspaper, as for the trivet on page 59 and the ends of the dowels of the dishrack on page 64.

Bevelled edges can look even more delicate. The plywood top and bottom of the sewing box on page 73 have bevelled edges, which is a nice decoration for an otherwise unattractive edge. Bevelling is easily done with a few strokes of a small blockplane. When cutting across end grain, plane in from both ends towards the middle to avoid the wood splitting at the corners.

For an even more professional look you can 'shape' the edges with an electric router which is easy to use. Refer to page 42 for instructions and safety hints on using the router.

You can buy inexpensive cutters for the router which will not only round or bevel the edges perfectly, but will also make coved, fluted and even rebated edges. Each cutter does one particular job and soon you will build up a variety of cutters much like a set of drill bits, to give you a wide choice in decorative touches.

You just run the router along the edge of the wood. The cutter itself usually has a small extension which runs along the edge to guide the cutter along. Push the router firmly along at the right speed and in the right direction so that the cutter cuts 'into' the wood.

If you are putting a moulded edge on all four sides, such as a drawer front for example, first cut across the ends and then along the sides, so that any wood which splits as you finish the cut

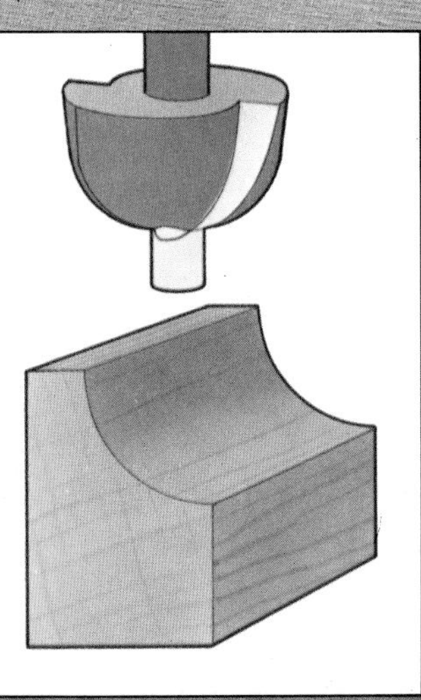

To give your work a really finished look, use router cutters to make decorative mouldings. The photograph shows some of the routers available and the shape of cut each makes. The detailed drawings of two cutters show the different types of effect you can achieve; the router on the left does

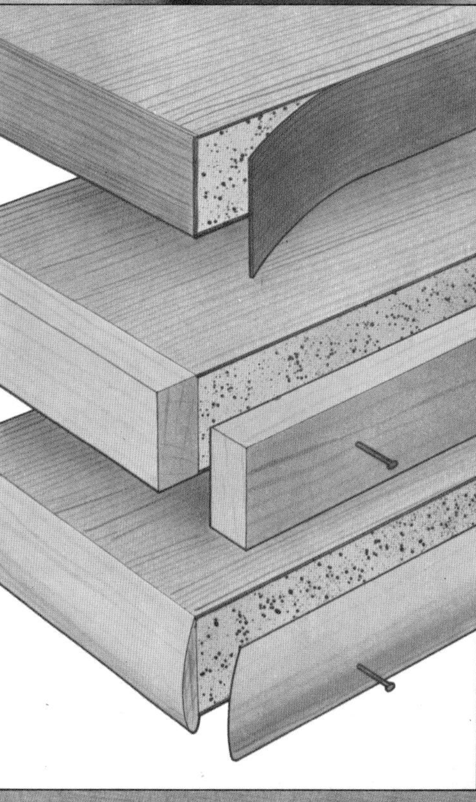

not give as wide a cut as the one on its right. (For detailed instructions on routing, see page 42.)
For finishing the edges of sheet materials use iron-on edging **(inset, right)**, *softwood strips or half-round moulding depending on the desired effect. The second two are nailed into place.*

along the edge is removed by the next cut.

With a bit of practice you can make your own mouldings for applying as decorative touches on doors and furniture, or for making your own picture frames. Make a simple moulding like this one out of any hardwood such as ramin, by making a first cut with a cove cutter and a second one with a rebate cutter.

Applying strips and mouldings

Plywood, blockboard and chipboard are quite inexpensive to work with. They are sold with beautiful veneered surfaces such as oak, mahogany or birch but the edges are always unsightly. There are various ways to cover the edges to give a neat professional finish. The easiest way is to use special iron-on edging strips. These can be bought from do-it-yourself shops in several woods, usually mahogany, teak or oak. They are made to match the surface veneers of the boards and come in standard widths. The glue on the back is the old-fashioned animal glue which melts when an iron is run along the surface and sets again in a few seconds as it cools.

Solid wood strips can also be nailed to the edges. These can be rectangular softwood strips, available in various thicknesses, or they can be mouldings. A very attractive shape is the half-round moulding which is available in widths from 9mm to about 25mm and can be nailed directly to the edges of sheet materials. Set the nails, fill the holes and sand smooth before finishing with paint or stain.

The shelf unit on page 61 can be made of less expensive chipboard instead of pine and painted red. Use half-round moulding to match or contrast with the unit.

There are various other moulding shapes which can be used as edging. See page 13.

Finishing

The workmanship and materials determine the value and usefulness of your project, but its final appearance will depend on the finish. This last step in your work deserves a great deal of planning and care so that the effort put into a project is not ruined by bad finishing.

A finish is applied to the surface of the wood to seal and protect it against moisture and light, and to enhance the surface or cover blemishes.

Less expensive woods and sheet materials are often finished with opaque finishes such as emulsion or gloss paint which cover blemishes and make the surface uniform and smooth. More expensive woods are finished with transparent finishes like polyurethane varnishes and oil wood stains which accent the beautiful grain patterns. The first step in finishing the wood is to prepare the surface by sanding it until it is smooth and even.

Sanding

Glasspaper is the most important finishing tool. Without it, no job is really complete. It is used to remove all the scratches and nicks caused while you are working the wood, leaving the surface smooth and even. The smoothness of the finish will depend on the fineness of the glasspaper. Glasspaper or sandpaper is coated with an abrasive which cuts the surface of the wood and smooths out all the rough spots. It is sold in many grades from very rough to extremely fine, and with a variety of abrasives. The higher the grit number, the finer the glasspaper is.

Glasspaper can be used across the grain for rough work, but the result will be a scratchy surface. For finished work, it is essential to sand *with* the grain. Begin with fairly coarse paper and then use progressively finer grades until you have achieved the finish you want. It is easier to sand if you wrap a convenient-sized piece of sandpaper around a small rectangular wooden block or purpose-made cork sanding block. This allows you to apply even pressure when you are sanding and it is not so rough on your hands. For sanding in rounded corners, wrap a small piece of sandpaper around a short length of dowel.

Hand sanding can be a tedious and time-consuming job, especially with hardwoods. Power sanders are useful for major sanding, but the final touches should be done by hand. It is very important that the final sanding is along the grain, avoiding circular or cross motions, otherwise the surface will be scratched and will have to be sanded again to get it smooth.

Immediately after sanding brush or wipe off the dust with a soft cloth or brush. For an even smoother surface, wipe it with a slightly damp rag or sponge to raise the grain of the wood. When the surface is once again dry, sand it once more with a very fine sandpaper.

The wood is now ready for an application of the protective finish.

Fillers and stoppers

If a board has cracks, splits or holes which need to be filled, or if you want to sink nails and screws and fill the holes so the surface is smooth, this can be done with plastic wood, putty, or polyfilla, depending on the kind of materials you are filling. Plastic wood compounds are available in a variety of wood colours and can therefore be used to fill flaws in many different woods. If the colour of the filler does not match the wood exactly, mix some of the filler with fine sawdust of the wood or add a few drops of wood stain. Apply the filler to the surface with a putty knife or spatula, allow to dry and then sand smooth.

There are other types of fillers used by professional woodworkers to fill the overall grain of the wood so that it is extremely smooth and will take a finish evenly. These come in paste or liquid form. Paste fillers are used for open-grained woods like oak, ash, walnut and mahogany, and liquid fillers for close-grain species like pine, maple and Douglas fir. For the home handyman, it is sufficient to sand a surface well before applying a finish.

Painting

Painting wood and sheet materials is a good way of hiding blemishes, and adding colour and creating accents in a project. (See the shelf project on page 76 for an example of how attractive a bright paint can be.) Once the surface is even and smoothed, paint will cover any imperfections.

It is a good idea to apply a primer coat to the surface, either an undercoat specially made for

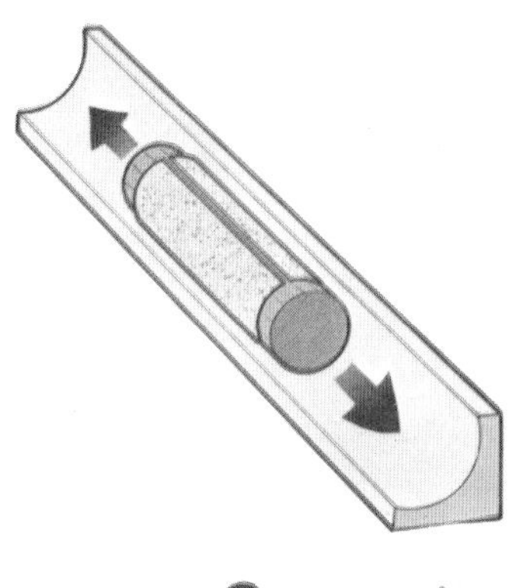

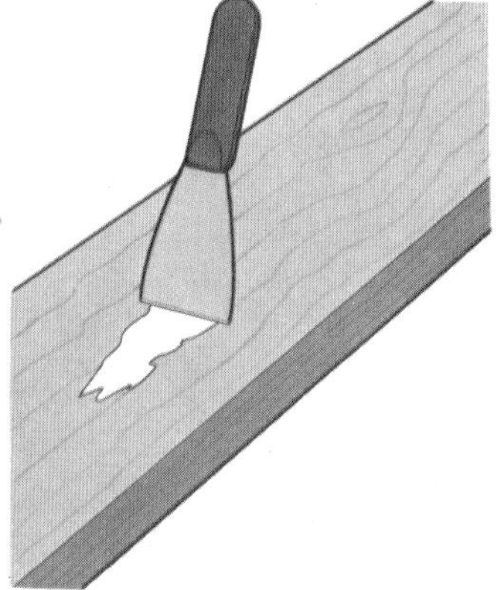

TOP: *Always sand with the grain and a sanding block for best results.*
CENTRE: *To sand grooves wrap sandpaper around a dowel.*
ABOVE: *Fill any cracks with filler and then sand smooth when it has dried.*
LEFT, FROM TOP RIGHT: *These Dylonwood stains show the wide range of wood finishes to choose from: pine (matt), Carmesine, sauna blue, pine (gloss), medium oak, red cedar, rosewood.*

the purpose or a sealer like a polyurethane varnish. This will provide a smooth base for the paint and reduce the amount of paint which sinks into the surface, making the finish more even. Allow the sealer enough time to dry thoroughly and sand it lightly before applying the first coat of paint. When painting sheet materials, at least two coats will be needed in addition to the undecoat to get a really even finish. Smooth the surface of chipboard and plywood by wiping it with a very watered-down solution of polyfilla and fill in the grain. Allow it to dry and sand it smooth.

Emulsion paints dry very quickly and are odour-free and therefore more pleasant to work with than gloss paints. An emulsion surface can be touched up and will dry a uniform colour, cutting out the need to repaint the whole surface. As emulsion paints are waterbased, brushes clean easily with soap and water. But as emulsion paints are fairly dull in finish and are not entirely waterproof, they are suitable only for indoor work.

Gloss paint provides a harder, more durable surface. It is, however, more difficult to apply evenly. It is essential to begin with a smooth surface and to apply an even undercoat before painting with gloss. Paint continuously in one direction going back over the areas covered to smooth out any drips or imperfections. Allow the paint enough time to dry if more than one coat is applied, sanding lightly between coats.

The advantage of finishing items in gloss paint is that you can wash them later with soap and water. Even though sometimes more attractive, emulsioned work is not as easy to clean.

Staining

A stain adds warm wood tones or bright colours to the wood without hiding the grain. It is used to protect the wood without hiding it. Inexpensive woods can be stained to look like a wide range of more exotic types from rosewood to walnut and teak. Stains are usually either oil or water based. Oil based stains give a more even finish for wood tones, but test the colour on a scrap of wood before starting, to decide if you like it and also to determine how many coats of stain are necessary. Before staining, wipe the surface with a damp rag to raise the grain, allow it to dry and then sand it smooth with very fine paper. In this way the surface will accept the stain evenly, without raising the grain. Apply the stain freely and quickly with a brush or cloth working with the grain. Avoid overlapping the strokes or the stain will be darker in some places. Apply at least two coats of stain for a rich finish, then apply a coat of clear varnish to bring out the richness of the grain.

Stains can also be used on sheet material. Plywood stains well in a range of wood tones like teak and oak, but choose the best side of the sheet to use as the face side. Chipboard too looks quite elegant in a variety of wood colours which bring out the texture of the surface.

Varnish

The most commonly used varnishes are polyurethane varnishes, available clear in matt, satin or gloss finishes and in a variety of colours, either wood tones or bright decorator colours. Polyurethane varnishes are extremely durable and resistant to water, alcohol, and other

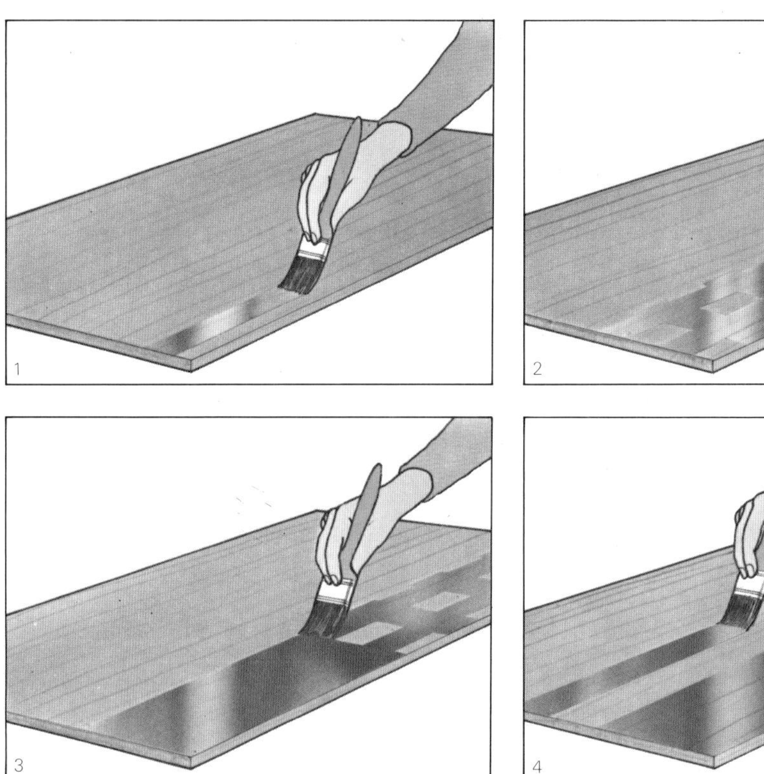

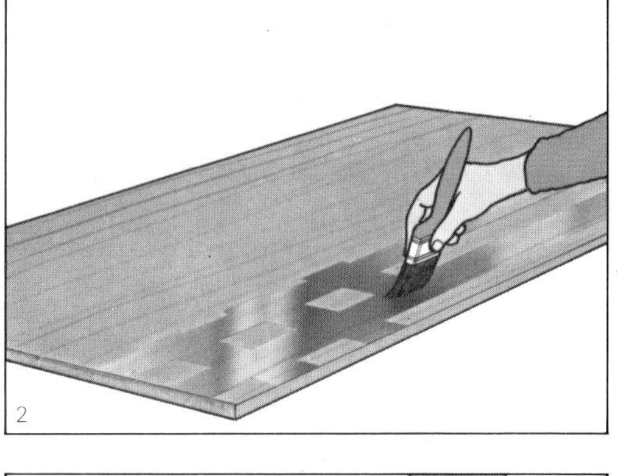

Varnishing is not a complicated task, but there is a correct way of doing it. By following this method, you should be guaranteed a smooth and even finish on every job. First apply the varnish in strips **(1)** *along the grain of the timber. Then brush across the grain* **(2)** *to fill in the areas and finally* **(3)** *brush lightly over the whole surface along the grain to smooth over the varnish. Repeat this procedure* **(4)** *for adjacent and remaining areas.*

solvents. They can be applied over wood stains or directly on to well-sanded wood for a warm, natural look. Brush on the varnish liberally with the grain, thinning down the first coat slightly with white spirit. Allow 24 hours for each coat to dry. Sand lightly with very fine glass paper between coats and wipe down with a damp rag. Apply at least two coats for a lustrous finish. For a matt finish, only the final varnish coat should be matt: the first coat should be gloss. After the final coat is rubbed down with fine wire wool, rub in a coat of wax for a really luxurious surface.

Polyurethane varnishes in wood tones eliminate the need for first staining and then varnishing the wood. Both operations are combined in one. Several decorator colours including blue, green and red are also available and look especially attractive on pine chipboard and plywood.

Brushes

Each type of finish uses a different solvent and it is therefore best to use a brush for only one type of finish. Mark the brush handles to indicate whether they are to be used for gloss paint, varnish, or emulsion paints.

Before using a brush, it is wise to clean it by shaking off any dust and washing it in turpentine or white spirit. Dry it off thoroughly before using.

The best brushes are made of natural bristle but they are very expensive. Nylon-bristle brushes are suitable for most jobs and cost a lot less. It is always a good idea to buy the best quality brush you can afford and to take very good care of it, rather than buy cheap brushes which will not last as long and do not give as smooth a finish.

Clean brushes thoroughly after use in the appropriate solvent and then wash in warm soapy water. Smooth the bristles in place and allow the brush to dry thoroughly. Keep the clean brushes wrapped in paper and stored flat.

Wax polishing

To achieve a really soft and satiny finish, the wood can be rubbed with wax. Both paste and liquid waxes are available and woodworkers mix their own waxes for each job. Several thin coats of wax well rubbed in with a soft cloth are better than one thick coat, as this allows the wax to soak into the wood. Wax can be applied on to the bare well-sanded wood or over stains or varnishes for a really luxurious finish. Buff each coat of wax vigorously with a soft cloth to bring out the full beauty of the wood.

Hand-rubbed finishes

If you have made a fine piece of furniture or used an especially beautiful piece of hardwood, it is worth the time and work to hand rub the finish. Two methods are useful for the home handyman. The surface of the wood can be rubbed with a very fine grade wire wool until it is glass smooth and then waxed, or it can be rubbed with a paste made of water and pumice powder, available from hardware shops, on a felt pad. Either method will smooth and polish the wood beautifully.

If the wood has been varnished, rubbing with the pumice compound will dull the surface and take away any lacquered look. The wood can then be waxed finally to give it an extra shine. There are other, professional, hand-rubbing methods such as French polishing which are complex and require specialist materials.

Oil finishing

An oil finish is an extremely simple and durable finish which is moderately resistant to heat and water and is therefore often used for dining tables. It suits several kinds of hardwood such as maple and teak.

Use ready-made teak oil or mix equal parts of linseed oil and turpentine and rub it into the surface of the wood. Teak oil is better, as it leaves no watermarks. Repeat the process once the oil has soaked in, wiping the excess off each time with a rag, to build up several coats. The finish penetrates into the wood and enhances the grain. The great advantage of an oil finish is that a portion of the surface can be reworked without refinishing the whole, as the oil blends readily into the wood. Renew the oil finish from time to time, depending on the kind of use the wood is getting. A teak draining board should be oiled every two months, and a maple dining table every three months.

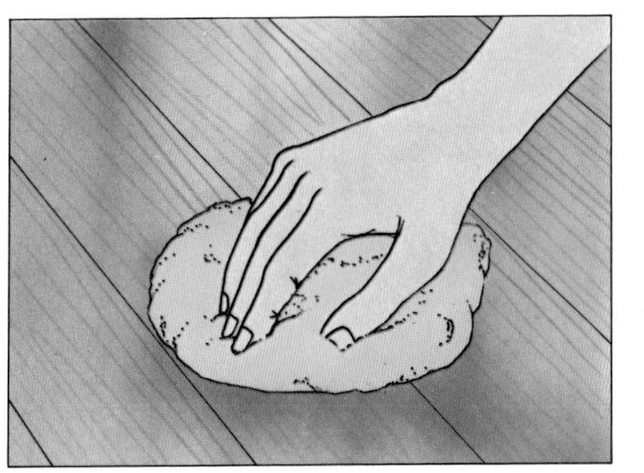

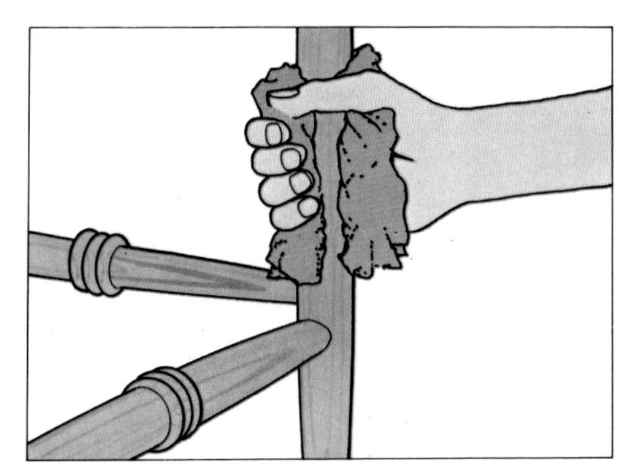

The key to a good oil or wax finish is several applications of thin coats as opposed to one thick coat. Apply oil or wax finishes with a soft, clean cloth and move your hand in a firm, circular motion. There is a wide range of waxes and oils you can use on wood; if in doubt, consult a timber merchant or furniture shop. For legs and other irregular shapes, rub (as shown) in an up and down movement, again with a soft cloth, making sure you cover the area completely.

Hardware

Metal hardware such as hinges, knobs, catches and locks are used for almost all furniture. Very often the choice of hardware such as the pulls on a chest of drawers is critical to the appearance of the piece. It is essential to fit an antique shaped and finished handle to an old fashioned chest, and a simple elegant one to a modern chest. Find out what is available by visiting large hardware shops which have the goods on display or send for catalogues from companies who specialise in the hardware you are looking for. Several mail order firms will send out free catalogues.

Hinges

The most commonly used pieces of hardware are hinges, for doors, cabinet flaps, and wherever else a folding action is required.

A door that is slightly smaller than the opening and fits neatly inside it is called a "flush" door. Another door is slightly larger than the opening and fits on the face of the frame, known as a "lay-on" door. There is a bewildering variety of hinges to suit either type of door, from the old fashioned butt hinges to the modern concealed cylinder hinges which can be fitted in minutes with special tools.

Most shops sell only a few of these hinges and the choice is generally easier. Furthermore, hardware merchants are usually very helpful and will advise you if you are in doubt about which type to use.

Butt hinge The most common hinge is the old fashioned butt hinge used on flush doors. There are many other hinges which are much easier to fit but the butt hinge always looks elegant and is extremely strong. It is available in many sizes and finishes such as steel, brass and chrome.

Hinges are measured first by the height of the leaf and second by the length of the entire hinge when opened. To fit a butt hinge, place the door in the opening, wedging it up a millimetre or so into its final position. Mark the exact location of the two hinges (three for a heavy house door) on both the frame and the door. The hinges should be positioned symmetrically a small distance in from either end.

Remove the door, mark the outline of the hinge leaf on both the door and the frame. The pivot of the hinges should project about halfway out from the edge. Score the pencil line with a trimming knife or chisel and then chop away a layer of wood with the chisel. The slot should be just the right depth so that the leaf fits exactly flush with the surface. If it is too high take out a bit more wood; if it is too low, pack it with a piece of cardboard.

Cut out all four recesses, mark the hole locations and drill the clearance and pilot holes for the screws. The screws should be the right weight so that the countersink head is flush with the hinge leaf. Usually a 19mm length is adequate for even the heaviest doors.

RIGHT: *A selection of brass fittings that are available from hardware or specialist shops including hinges, door knobs, latches of various descriptions, finger plates and decorative screws.*

As doors vary, so do the hinges on which they swing.
BELOW: *Five types of hinges. Butt hinge* **(1)**. *Lift-off hinge* **(2)**. *Pivot hinge* **(3)**. *Cranked hinge* **(4)**. *Continuous, or piano, hinge* **(5)**.

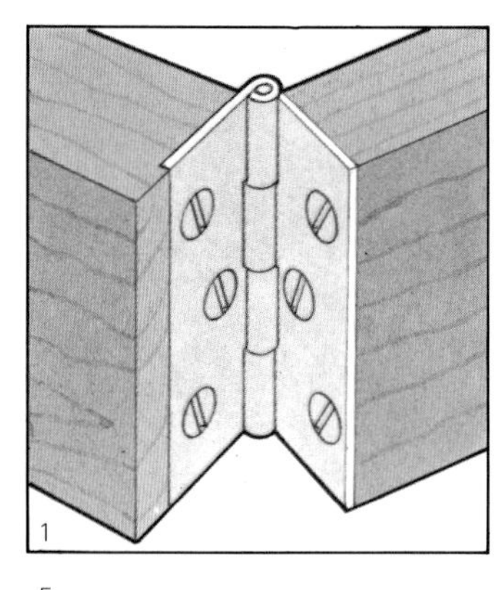

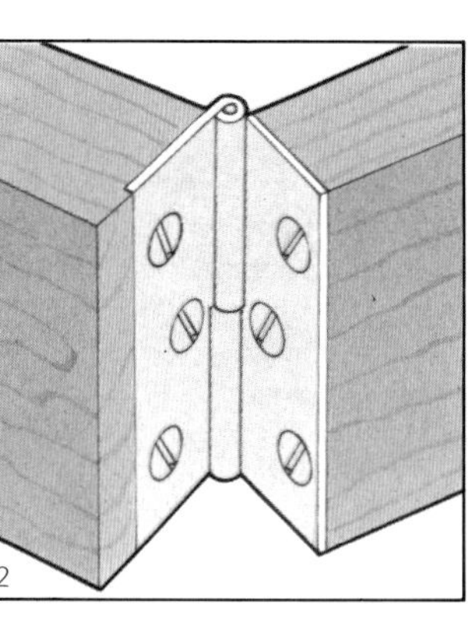

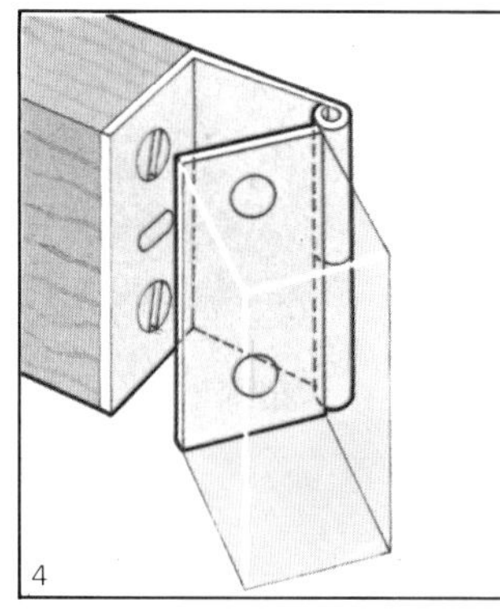

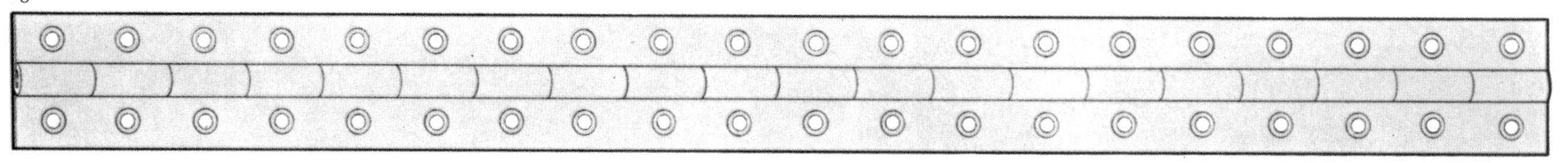

To fit a hinge first mark the outline of the leaf on the door (as shown) and then on the door frame.

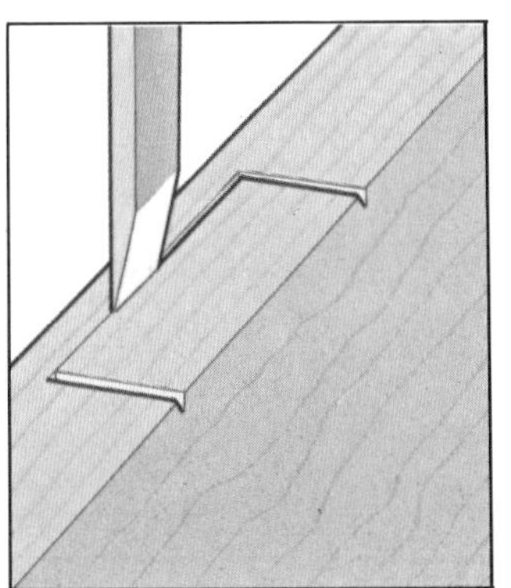

Score the marked line with a trimming knife or sharp chisel so that you can chisel away the wood within the lines to the required shape.

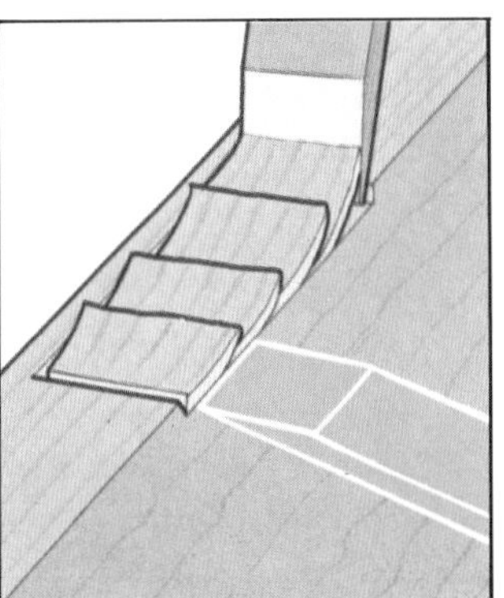

Make a recess to just the right depth so that the hinge is flush with the surface of the wood.

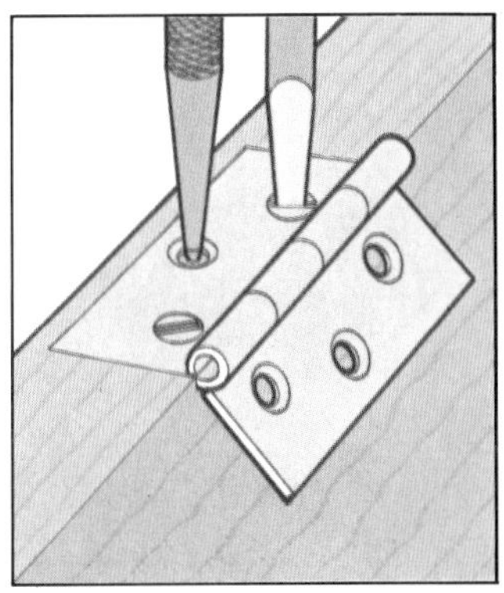

Finally, mark the position of the screw with a pencil or other sharp implement so that the hinge can be screwed into place to finish.

Screw the hinges to the door first, then hold the door open on its wedges as you screw the hinges to the frame. Try the door with only one screw in each hinge to make sure it fits correctly. Adjust if necessary and add the remaining screws. This is a crucial stage, so be absolutely sure the alignment is correct.

Lift-off hinge The lift-off hinge is very easy to fit and extremely convenient because it separates into two parts, allowing the door to be lifted off.

The two halves can be fitted to the frame and door separately, the door brought in position and lifted in place. The small brass variety is especially useful for lay-on kitchen cabinet doors. It is both attractive and practical, as it allows the doors to be removed for easier access for cleaning.

Pivot hinge Pivot hinges are very easy to fix. They fit on the top and bottom edges of lay-on doors. These hinges are called 180° hinges: they allow the cabinet doors to open a full 180° flat against an adjoining door.

Cranked hinge The cranked hinge is also used for lay-on doors. It is generally available in several varieties either for a 9, 12 or 15mm thick door. Use it like the pivot hinge for cabinets with several adjacent doors. It allows the door to open clear of the adjacent door. It does have the disadvantage that it is visible on the outside edge of the door.

Continuous or piano hinge The continuous hinge has many uses besides its traditional use to support the piano cover. It is readily available in lengths up to 1.8m in either brass finish, aluminium or plastic.

Cut it off to the length required with a hacksaw and screw it directly to the surface. Because it is continuous with closely spaced screw fittings it is quite strong and reliable. Use it as a quick fitting hinge on cabinet doors, lids, and wherever else two long edges need to be hinged together. The simple trestles on page 45 consist of two pieces of chipboard connected at the top edge with a length of continuous hinge.

Knobs and handles

Most doors and drawers require some form of knob or handle. These come in a wide variety of shapes, sizes and materials. Consult a specialist firm if you require a particular handle to match a cabinet.

For most uses a simple metal or wooden handle is sufficient. The handles either have a single screw fixing from the front, requiring a small pilot hole, or they are fitted with bolts from the inside of the drawer or door.

The small brass knob is a popular fixing for small cabinet doors. It is fairly inexpensive and available in several sizes. To fit it, drill a small pilot hole and turn the knob to screw it firmly in place.

Wooden knobs are also very popular. You can buy quite elaborate turned ones either new in the shops or old ones in street markets or antique shops. Simple pine handles go very well on bureaus and chests. They can be painted or left natural.

You can also make handles. For the small sewing box on page 73, for example, a wooden ball was screwed onto the lid as a handle. Make pulls for small drawers out of lengths of stripping with holes drilled at regular intervals. Cut the handles off with one central hole for a pull and attach it by screwing it on from the back.

Locks and catches

All cabinet doors require a stop and catch to keep them closed, and there are many kinds of catches available.

The two easiest and most reliable types are the magnetic catch and the ball catch.

The magnetic catch has two parts. The part holding the magnet is screwed the correct distance back inside the cabinet. The plate screws to the back of the door and is fitted so that it just touches the magnet to keep the door closed. The magnet part has slotted holes to allow minor adjustment. Make sure that the door fits flush and is held firmly closed by the magnet.

The ball catch has a spring loaded ball which springs out to locate in the recess in the frame. It is available in both plastic and metal versions and in many sizes from the small kitchen cabinet size to the large ones required for full-sized doors.

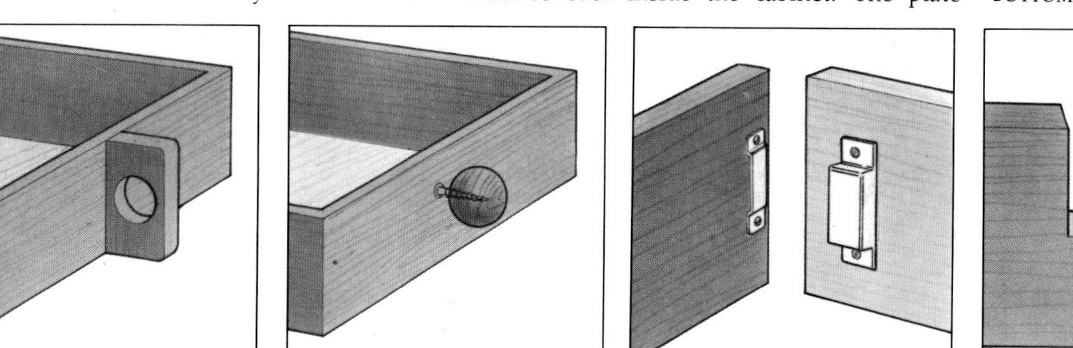

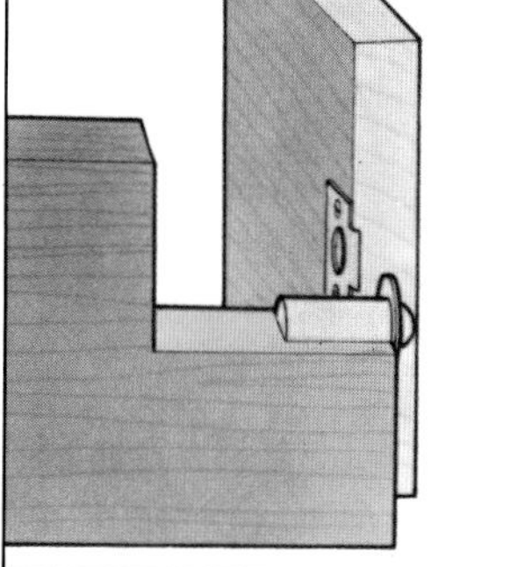

BELOW, FROM LEFT: *You can make original pulls for drawers with offcuts of wood into which a circular hole has been drilled or with bought wooden balls screwed in place. For keeping doors securely shut, the magnetic catch is easy to install and allows for adjustment after it has been screwed in. The ball catch, another shutting device, is available in a range of sizes for different purposes.*

BOTTOM: *A plate-fitting castor.*

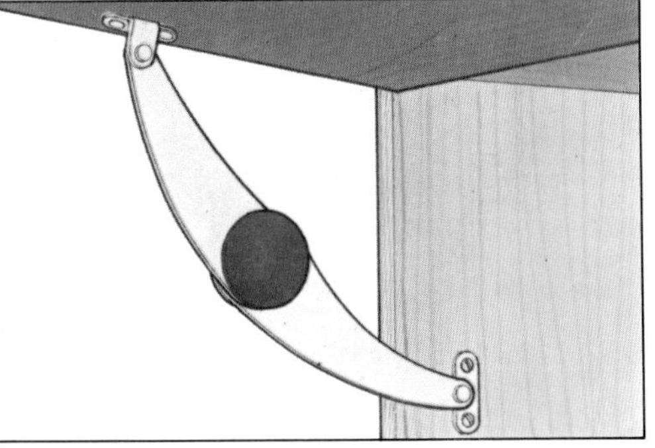

TOP: *There is an ever-growing selection of decorative brass hardware, in both modern and antique styles. Older furniture, such as this pine chest, is usually better suited to antique-type fittings.*

ABOVE LEFT: *The drop flap is both convenient and sturdy, and easy to fix to a cabinet.*

ABOVE RIGHT: *The lift-up stay is useful for doors that need to be held open for lengthy periods.*

Miscellaneous fittings

Drop flaps and lift up doors require stays to keep them open in position. For drop flaps, as used on a drinks cabinet for example the sliding flap stay is a fairly new and ingenious device. The cupboard end of the stay slides up and down on a channel, instead of moving into the cupboard. This saves space inside the cupboard. It is usually secured to the door, and to the cabinet with short chrome raised-head screws.

The lift up stay is used for doors or flaps which are hinged at the bottom and opened upwards. The doors above a wardrobe, for example, often open upward. The stay holds the door open leaving you with both hands free to get things in and out.

Castors Castors are small wheels which are fitted on the bottom of furniture to enable it to be moved around. They are usually fitted, in sets of four, to the bottoms of legs or under the corners of drawers.

The type and size of castor required will depend on the weight it has to carry and how invisible you want it to be. The castors for the toy bins on page 78, for example, can be a basic inexpensive type as they are hidden away under the bin.

There are two types of castors. The plate-fixing type is screwed to the underside of the furniture whereas the grip-neck type fixes into a socket which has been hammered into a pre-drilled hole.

Castors can sometimes leave unsightly marks on the carpeting underneath. If this occurs, you should, if it is possible, move the piece of furniture to another part of the room.

Glossary

A

abrasive: material used for smoothing wood, includes glasspaper, wire wool.
animal glue: adhesives made from animal waste, often called scotch glue, sold in flake or powder form, and must be heated to be used.
annual ring: the difference in colour between spring and summer wood growth produces an annual ring; these rings are seen in cross sections of trunks.
architrave: decorative moulding framing a door or window.
auger bit: rotating cutting tool used in brace to drill holes.
awl: a sharp pointed small tool used mainly for making small pilot holes in timber.

B

batten: narrow strip of timber used to cover an edge or support shelves.
beading: small convex moulding shape used to decorate and cover edges.
bench hook: a bench aid made of a board and two battens screwed together and used in place of a vice to hold a piece of wood while it is being sawed.
bench stop: steel or wooden device that fits into a hole on workbench and is used to brace boards as they are planed.
bevel: to cut the edge of a board at an angle.
bit: a rotating cutting tool used in brace, hand-drill or drillpress to bore holes. Types include auger bits, expansion bit and twist drills.
blemish: an imperfection which detracts from the appearance of wood but does not affect its strength.
blockboard: sheet material made of series of core strips glued together side by side to form a slab, sandwiched between layers of veneer.
block plane: all-purpose plane with small blade set at a low angle for use in cutting across grain, also used for bevelling edge of timber.
bolt: a type of fitting used to fasten wood to wood and wood to other materials. Used with a nut which screws onto the threaded shank.
brace: a hand tool for boring holes. A chuck at the bottom holds auger bits.
bracket: a piece of metal or wood joined at an angle, used as a support.
bradawl: a pointed steel tool with wooden handle used to make a hole to start a screw.
butt hinge: most common type of hinge, with either a fixed or a loose pin.
butt joint: simple joint in which two pieces of wood are placed against each other but held with nails, screws, dowels, glue or other fasteners.

C

calipers: instrument for precise measuring inside and outside dimensions of round, oval and irregular objects difficult to measure with a rule.
casein glue: glue made from milk and sold as powder to be mixed with water. Water resistant but not waterproof.
castor: a wheel fixed to the bottom of furniture so that it can be rolled about.
centre punch: a pointed steel tool used with hammer to make starting holes for screws and drill bits.
chamfer: to remove the sharp corner along the edge of a board by planing to a 45° angle.
check: a horizontal crack in a piece of wood as a result of shrinkage during drying.
chipboard: a man-made sheet material with rough texture made of woodchips bonded together under pressure. Resists warping and shrinkage. Used for construction work, table-tops and as base for veneers.
chisel: rigid wood or plastic handled tool with straight cutting edge used for removing wood with or across the grain. Chisels are worked either by hand pressure or by striking the end of the handle with a wooden mallet.
circular saw: a portable power saw with revolving blade used for ripping or crosscutting. It is especially useful for cutting large sheet materials.
claw hammer: fairly large head hammer with two prongs on head for pulling nails.
clearance hole: hole drilled in wood to accept the shank of a screw.
combination square: measuring device with a steel handle which slides along the base. Useful not only for marking right angles but also for making longitudinal lines on boards and for finding the depth of holes.

compass saw: a thin-bladed saw, used for cutting small holes or curves in wood, also called a keyhole saw.
contact adhesive: synthetic glue that forms a tight bond without cramping. Used for plastic laminates, chipboard and hardboard.
coping saw: hand saw consisting of U-shaped steel frame fitted with slender blade used for cutting irregular shapes in thin wood and plywood.
countersink: to sink the heads, screws or bolts flush with or slightly below the surface of the timber using a countersinking drill bit.
crosscut saw: a hand saw with fine teeth used for cutting across the grain of wood.
cross-pein hammer: lightweight hammer with small head used for nailing panel pins and small nails.

D

defect: a defect in timber is an imperfection which affects the strength or usability of the wood, for example a split or crack.
depth stop: collar or marker fitted over a drill bit to control the depth of drilling.
dovetail joint: attractive joint used for drawers and in fine furniture with interlocking teeth.
dowel: a round piece of wood frequently used in furniture and making wood dowel joints.
dowelling jig: a device to simplify the drilling of holes in pieces of wood to make dowel joints.
drill: a hand tool used for drilling small holes. Types include the hand drill and the breast drill.
drill stand: a steel stand on which a portable electric drill is mounted so that it is worked like a drill press.

E

end grain: grain exposed when a piece of wood is cut across, called cutting across the grain.
escutcheon: small plate used to cover keyhole, fixed with round headed escutcheon pins or with screws.

F

face: the prepared side of the timber chosen as the best side. Traditionally marked with a pencil line in a loop.
fence: guide attached to a plane or power saw to guide the tool a fixed distance from the edge of the work. For example, rip fence for a circular saw.
figure: the grain pattern of the wood as exposed by sawing.
file: hand tool used to shape or smooth wood or metal.
flush: forming a smooth level surface.

G

gimlet: boring tool like small auger, but with wooden handle.
glass paper: abrasive paper used for smoothing and finishing wood by rubbing. Graded according to coarseness. Used by hand or in a power sander.
G-cramp: so named because of its shape. Useful small clamp with adjustable bolt through one end.
gouge: chisel-like cutting tool with rounded or U-shaped cutting edge. Used for digging out wood and making grooves or carving. Used in same way as chisels.
grain: direction in which fibres on piece of wood run, and the resulting pattern.
green wood: wood which is unseasoned and therefore not as strong or stable as dried wood.
grinding angle: angle ground on blade of plane or chisel from which the cutting edge is sharpened.
groove: channel cut along the length of a piece of wood, parallel with the grain.

H

hardboard: hard and strong man-made sheet material made of compressed wood fibres sold in large panels in thicknesses of 4mm and 6.5mm. Used mainly for inexpensive cabinet work.
hardwood: misleading term referring to timber of trees with broad leaves. Generally more expensive and harder wearing wood, such as mahogany and oak.
heart shake: split across the centre of a log.
heartwood: mature inner wood of a log, usually darker than the surrounding wood.
honing: sharpening plane or chisel blade to the honing angle, slightly greater than the grinding angle.
housing joint: joint consisting of a groove usually cut across the grain into which the end of another member is housed or fitted to form the joint.

I

inlay: to set small pieces of wood or other material into a surface for decorative purposes.
invisible hinge: hinges which are completely concealed when installed. Used mainly in cabinet doors.

J

jack plane: all-purpose plane used for trimming and smoothing wood.
jigsaw: portable power saw fitted with straight narrow blade which moves up and down in short strokes. Used for cutting irregular shapes and for making holes.

K

kerf: the narrow width cut through wood by the saw blade.
key: to roughen adjacent surfaces prior to gluing or finishing with paint to improve adhesion.
kiln-dried timber: timber dried in controlled conditions in a large oven called a kiln.
knots: remnants of branches in timber considered to be defects because they can reduce the strength of the wood and detract from its appearance.

L

laminate: to glue together layers or plies of wood, usually under pressure. The process by which plywood is made.
lap joint: joint where the whole of one member is fitted into a matching cut-out in the other member.
log: the portion of a tree trunk which is used for boards.

M

mallet: wooden hammering tool with wide-faced head designed to minimise damage to object being struck.
marking gauge: a rule-like device with a sharp pin at one end of a wooden bar which can slide up and down the bar and be set firmly. Used to mark lines parallel with planed edge of timber.
mitre: to cut at a 45° angle as in mitre joint.
mitre box: a bench aid to simplify cutting mitres with slots set at exactly 45° into which the saw fits.
mitre cramps: cramps used in sets of four to hold the corners of a mitred frame square.
moulding: a strip of wood cut into decorative shapes used to cover joints, serve as decoration or other practical functions. Types include half round, ogee and quadrant.
mortise and tenon joint: a very strong joint which is formed by a tongue-like piece or tenon. The tenon then fits into a mortise or slot cut into a second piece.

N

nail: a standard fastener in carpentry not much used in woodworking as it is not as strong or permanent as a screw, dowel or glue join. Types include oval nail, panel pin.
nail punch: small rigid steel punch with concave tip used to sink nails below the surface of the wood.
nominal size: the size of a section of timber before it is planed down to its working size. Timber is sold according to the sawn or nominal size, planed timber is a couple of millimetres smaller in width and thickness.

O

oilstone: a stone used for sharpening cutting tools, treated with oil to prevent steel particles from clogging the pores of the stone.
orbital sander: a sophisticated power sanding device which works by vibration and which produces an exceptionally high-quality finish.

P

Phillips head screw/screwdriver: screw with cross slot in simple star shape driven by matching screwdriver.
piano hinge: a long continuous hinge which can be cut off to the length required. Used for piano tops, heavy table leaves and cabinet doors.
pilot hole: hole drilled in timber to receive the threaded shank of a screw or large nail which might otherwise split the wood.
pincers: a tool similar to pliers, with jaws for pulling nails or hooks.
plane: tool for smoothing rough surfaces or making timber level, or for cutting rebates.
plug cutter: small tool used in a powerdrill to cut out matching wood plugs to cover screw heads or to fill holes.
plywood: strong, durable and stable man-made sheet material made of three or more layers of veneer laminated together. Sold in standard sheets in thicknesses from 4mm to 25mm.
Pozidriv screw/screwdriver: screw with cross slot shaped in double star which must be driven by matching screwdriver.
PVA glue: all-purpose woodworking glue made of an emulsion of polyvinyl acetate in water.

Q

quarter round: simple moulding shaped like a quadrant used to cover joints between floor and skirting and in inside corners of furniture.
quarter sawn: wood cut from the logs in cuts along the radius like slices from a cake. The result is boards which are less likely to warp than boards cut 'through and through'.

R

rasp: similar to a file but with coarse teeth. Used to shape wood and round corners and edges.
rebate: rectangular groove or recess in the edge of a board, which holds panel or glass in a door or picture or frame.
rip saw: saw designed to cut along the grain.
router: versatile power tool used to make joints, cut grooves, mortise, rout out areas and shape edges.
rule: measuring tool used in woodworking most commonly as a steel tape rule.

S

sander: portable power tool which vibrates rapidly. Designed to give final finish to timber and sheet materials. Fitted with abrasive paper. Types include belt sander and orbital sander.
sanding block: device made of cork or wood to hold sandpaper for hand finishing.
sap: the life fluid of the tree, which is a gummy pitch in softwoods.
sapwood: young wood just inside the bark of trunk or branch, less dense than heartwood.
sash cramp: cramp used for work, up to about 2m long. It is an adjustable steel bar with a bolt at one end and a fixed jaw at the other, for cramping boards into table tops and joined frameworks.
sawset: tool used by 'sawdoctor' for bending saw teeth to left or right so saw will not stick.
screw: wood screws usually made of threaded steel or brass, used to join wood to wood or wood to other materials. Available in varying lengths and thicknesses and with different slot patterns in the head.
screwdriver: tool for turning screws, made of steel shank with plastic or wooden handle.
set: the bending of saw teeth alternately to one side and to the other along the blade.
shake: a lengthwise split between growth rings in timber.
sharpening stone: also called an oilstone, a special type of stone used for sharpening tools.
shoulder: step cut at end of wood to expose end grain, as in a tenon.
softwood: timber from trees with needle-shaped leaves, such as pine and spruce.
smoothing plane: all-purpose plane used for straightening pieces of timber.
spirit level: metal or wooden bar with glass bubble containing alcohol used to test the level or vertical of a surface.
square: L-shaped device used for checking the squareness of timber and for measuring and marking right angles.
stopping: purpose-made wood filler available in various wood shades including white. For filling small holes in wood before finishing.

T

template: shape used for repeated processes.
tenon: a projection found on the end of a piece of wood which is then inserted in a mortise of the same size, for making very strong joints.
tenon saw: small cross cut saw with the top of the blade stiffened with a piece of brass or steel, used for accurate small work.
tongue and groove: a board with a projecting rib or tongue along one long side and a channel or groove along the other in a corresponding position. The tongue of one board is designed to fit into the groove of the adjoining board, thus creating a rigid continuous surface.
try-square: L-shaped measuring tool with blade and handle used for testing wood for squareness and smoothness and for marking 90° lines on boards.

U

utility knife: knife with razor-like blade which protrudes from the handle. Useful for marking, cutting through veneers, etc.

V

veneer: very thin sheet of wood, sometimes exotic hardwood. Usually glued to a base of chipboard or blockboard.
vice: metal device for holding wood stationary while it is worked on at the workbench.

W

warp: a bend or twist in a piece of wood resulting from the uneven shrinkage of wood cells during seasoning.

Index

Acknowledgments

All photography by John Cook except page 91 — Elizabeth Whiting.

Jacket photography by Robert Golden.

Illustrations by Brian Watson, David Bryant and Terry Allen Design Limited/Lyn Brooks, Robert Burns, Roger Courthold, Robert Stoneman.

The publishers would also like to thank the following for kindly lending their products to be used for photography. E. Ammette & Co. Ltd., Pentonville Road, London N1 for all tools and equipment except: Black & Decker Ltd. for the portable electric router page 43; John Lewis for the spice jars on page 61; Sanderson Ltd. for wallpaper on pages 69 and 76; Dylon for preparing finishes on page 84; Timber Research and Development Assn., High Wycombe, Bucks. for timber sample pages 10-11; Record Ridgway Tools, Sheffield for benchstop and large vice page 37.